Music Lessons
That Are
Easy to Teach

Also by Jane L. Reynolds ....

MUSIC LESSONS YOU CAN TEACH

Music Lessons That Are Easy to Teach

JANE L. REYNOLDS

PARKER PUBLISHING COMPANY, INC.
WEST NYACK, NEW YORK

CIrc
Muac

© 1976 by

Parker Publishing Company, Inc.
West Nyack, New York

Library of Congress Cataloging in Publication Data

Reynolds, Jane L
  Music lessons that are easy to teach.

  Includes bibliography and index.
  1. Music--Manuals, text-books, etc. 2. School music
--Instruction and study--United States. I. Title.
MT10.R45   781   76-79
ISBN 0-13-608059-6

Printed in the United States of America

For the people who inspired this book—
the teachers and the children

WHAT THIS BOOK CAN DO FOR YOU

One of the continual concerns of educators is how to provide elementary school children with enough music lessons. The music specialist who meets with them once or twice a week regrets that his time is limited. Since young children are enthusiastic about making music and, since it can benefit them in countless ways, they deserve the chance to enjoy it as often as possible.

With this book you can have music with your children frequently, perhaps every day. Here are some of the ways you can fit fragments of lessons into a full schedule:

- Have "Singing Show and Tell."
- Ask children to improvise songs.
- Lead the class in scale practice.
- Conduct rehearsals of songs, song plays, etc., for performance.
- Have children dramatize music about the movements of animals, people at work, trains and other vehicles, toys, etc.
- Have the class sing a few rounds to put everyone in a good mood or to liven up the atmosphere.
- Show children how to sing patriotic (and other) songs with harmony.
- Have everyone make his or her own rhythm instruments.
- Have daily practice on melody instruments—recorders or whatever instruments the children are learning to play.
- Show children how to improvise on melody instruments.

These are just a few of the ideas for music activities which you can extract from this book.

The book should be helpful to anyone who feels insecure about his ability to teach music. Some of you may be concerned because you have had little or no formal training. Perhaps you feel you have little, if any, musical talent—you doubt that you can sing and you wonder if you know whether or not harmonized singing is in tune; to you a bassoon sounds like a tuba; and, since you have always been the one who was out of step in a march, it seems doubtful to you that you could have your children play rhythmically on rhythm instruments.

This book has been written to give you confidence that you can teach music. When technical knowledge is needed, you are told exactly what to do and how to do it. If material must be presented in a particular way, you are given words to read—actual questions to ask the children and answers that would be acceptable.

For example, the book shows you .....

- How to guide children to improvise songs
- How to help children create and write their own songs
- How to create song plays using original songs
- How to encourage children to dramatize songs and music
- How to lead children to create dances that interpret musical compositions
- How to have children chant words as rounds
- How to teach rounds to children of different abilities
- How to make harmony by singing harmonious songs together
- How to harmonize a song with an ostinato
- How to make chords with voices and use them to accompany songs
- How to make inexpensive rhythm instruments
- How to use rhythm instruments in various ways
- How to construct and play a one-stringed instrument
- How to give lessons on a wind instrument such as the recorder
- How to play melodies on percussion instruments such as the xylophone, resonator bells, etc

While the music specialist may know a lot about music and be able to perform it to some degree, you have the advantage of knowing your particular group of children intimately. You know what motivates them, how to elicit response from them, how to give them the self-assurance they need to participate, and how to guide their learning. In other words, you already know how to teach; this book gives you information for teaching music.

The first time you are to teach music with this book, hunt through it carefully until you find an idea for a lesson that you think you could teach well, one that your children would enjoy. Make it a personal choice, and avoid selecting anything you sense might give you difficulty. If the lesson goes well, you will prove to yourself that teaching music can be easy. Choose more ideas with which you feel comfortable; let one success lead to another. If your children are enthusiastic, their enthusiasm will boost your self-confidence. Soon you will look forward to having music.

Yes, music lessons *can* be easy to teach.

Jane L. Reynolds

CONTENTS

Part One

LESSONS IN

MUSICAL CREATIVITY

The ability which distinguishes human beings from other animals is the ability to create something new out of existing materials. This ability requires the use of a special kind of intelligence which is, for the most part, missing in other animals. Like them, people have instincts, needs, drives, and certain built-in response mechanisms such as the mechanism of blinking the eyes when something irritates or disturbs them. But it is man's ability to create and invent that has been the most useful in changing the quality of life on our planet.

The urge to create is strong in people of all ages. When the infant discovers that he has transformed his environment by accidentally scattering a pile of papers on the floor, he may try to repeat the action if the result has pleased him. When a homemaker changes the appearance of his house by painting it with a paint color which he has chosen, when a person creates a garment which changes his appearance, using cloth and pattern that he has selected—such people are behaving creatively in the same way as do professional artists, craftsmen, research scientists, etc.

A person can feel greatly rewarded by his creative behavior. The first rewarding feeling comes when he is getting the idea, and continues as he figures out what he is going to do. After the project is completed, if the result pleases him, the person may feel a second reward—a feeling of pride and satisfaction. And, when other people applaud what the creator has done, he may feel rewarded in the form of praise or approval.

As children, people are usually unabashed as they make attempts to be creative. But, too often, as grownups, the same people try to bottle up or deny these feelings. Of course, the need to create never goes away. It is not just the experts—master artists like da Vinci and master composers like Beethoven—who should be the creators. Anyone who has ever penned a letter can write a story; anyone who has sketched with pencil or crayons can make a picture; and anyone who has sung a song can create music.

Creating Music

The job of making a musical composition is similar to any other kind of creative work. Whether the composer is experienced and perhaps famous or an amateur composing for the first time, much time must be spent on trial and error. An "inspired" work only appears to come without effort. It is actually the result of much conscious and subconscious thought. Ideas may have been developing in the back of the mind of the creator for a long time, whether he was aware of them or not.

The music which each person creates will express his personality. As every teacher who has taught for any length of time knows, each class is distinctive and has its own character, although each individual may differ greatly from the others. A song can be written by a group and still express that group's "personality."

If you do not know the meaning of the symbols of music and cannot read them, do not be deterred from having your class make up songs. "Composing" need not mean writing notes. Children can have practice in composition every day in the form of impromptu improvisations. Also, everyone can participate in creating short songs of only two to four lines. If the music is not written, it can be memorized if everyone sings it a number of times on the day on which it is composed. To trigger the memory of it, the children and you could devise a method of "writing" the music. The words of a song will often help you recall the tune.

Creating to Music

Children can be led to create their own responses to existing musical compositions. This can mean that they will pantomime or dramatize songs, make body motions that show what an orchestral composition is about, create a dance in the rhythm of the music, or move their hands as if conducting an orchestra. Whatever the activity, the performer must hear what the music commands him to do and obey those commands.

Responding to music is natural, for people find that most music compels them to move. Its powers have been known and used throughout history. Marches have been played to help men try to win battles; music has been used as therapy for sick people. At the present time music is used to help sell products on radio and television; it is used in movies to help set the emotional tone. Countries have national songs, and religious sects have hymns. Those who use music to influence people know that human response to it is natural.

Benefits from Creating

When there is so much good music which you and your children could reproduce and so many existing dances which they could do, why should you ask them to create songs and respond to music? The answer is that the purpose in having lessons in musical creativity is not to compete with professional composers, dancers, etc. When people are inhibited by experts, they miss many benefits which come from creating.

The person who attempts something on his own, something original, becomes more aware than ever of how other people do or have done the same thing. The person who plans to knit a sweater or build a coffee table or write a poem looks with new interest at the sweaters, coffee tables, or poems others have made.

Your children, knowing they will be composing a song, will automatically look for ideas from other songs and from the music they hear. They will appreciate good music and be critical of that which is cheap or inferior.

Creating music or creating to music requires a special kind of thinking. The creator is always asking himself questions like the chess player pondering the consequences of his moves. "If I do this, it will leave that area open. If I make that move, the consequences are better . . . . . "

The person who creates a song sets up a lot of what will follow in the beginning. In the first phrase of the music the tempo is established, as well as the rhythm pattern, the note patterns of the melody, the general character of the piece. The composer contemplates what would happen if he changed the melody pattern, used other rhythms, a different tempo, another mode. After much experimenting he feels great satisfaction when he makes his decision about how to begin. Succeeding phrases of the song seem to fall into place, to take their shape from the first phrase.

In a similar way the creator of the interpretation of a piece of music with some kind of body motions must experiment until he finds the ones that seem right to him. By concentrating, listening intently to the music, the performer can succeed. Though the music directs him, he moves to it in his own unique way.

After he has tried composing, the amateur hears the compositions of others with greater appreciation. After he has had to listen carefully to the music he interprets with his body, the performer learns to be aware of all aspects of that music. Lessons in musical creativity are among the most valuable of all music lessons.

Chapter 1

YOU CAN TEACH COMPOSITION

It is as natural for an infant who is learning to use his voice to sing tones and make up tunes as it is for him to make the sounds of vowels and consonants. We hear the baby in the crib carrying on tests—holding tones, cutting them off sharply, cooing softly one moment, screaming loudly on a pitch the next, and so on. Every normal child in every part of the world experiments with all kinds of vocal sounds, teaching himself what he needs to know to make his voice talk or sing. In these play experiences he naturally uses the various components of singing.

Children are not usually expected to develop this natural ability to sing and compose vocal music. People who raise them encourage them to learn to speak words, but the interest in singing and making up music remains quite strong in every child. When you ask children to compose their own music, you will be asking them to revive a strong interest from the recent past.

A vocal composition can be simple, or it can be complex. It can be as short as two lines or phrases, sung by a single voice. It can be an intricate polyphonic piece with several voices and interweaving melodies. There is a considerable difference between the simple folk song, music from light operettas, church hymns and the like, and the more serious operas, the solemn and lengthy oratorios and cantatas.

Most young children are exposed to the simpler music— popular songs of the day, commercials for advertising, songs on television, etc. Such music is not only familiar; it is easy to understand and to learn. For these reasons, the songs your children compose will probably imitate the style of such music.

With this chapter to help you, you have a choice of guiding your children through a short course—perhaps asking them only to improvise songs. Or, you can expect them to move step-by-step to learn how to use the alphabet of music—the scale—and a musical vocabulary of scale segments with which to record their compositions. The person who knows how to write in the language of music has a means for communicating with everyone else who reads and writes the symbols of music.

IMPROVISATION

The ability to compose music without preparation or previous thought comes naturally to young children. This ability never leaves us, and older children also will find improvisation an enjoyable exercise.

Singing Show and Tell   (For Grades 1-3)

This exercise can be used daily in the classroom. It can serve to prepare students for creating more formal and longer compositions.

Have your children had experience in expressing themselves verbally to their classmates? If they have, tell them that you would like them to have "Singing Show and Tell." Participants must sing, rather than talk, about subjects. The topics would be the same—statements about the visit of a friend, about the money the Tooth Fairy left under the pillow, about the new shoes worn to school, about the new puppy at home, about any exciting events of the recent past.

Since most Show and Tell stories are spoken in just one or two sentences, you may find when these are sung that the music does not sound finished. For the most part it is advisable to accept almost any tune. The major requirement should be that the singers tell with their singing voices exactly what they would if they were talking.

If corrections are needed, try to have the children themselves be the critics, recognize problems and correct them. They may be bothered by the tune that stays on one tone, the tune that is too high in pitch, the one that is too low, the tune that lacks rhythmic organization, the tune that does not seem to end.

If a problem persists, tactfully suggest that the child try again. To the child who sings on a monotone say: "Make your voice move up and down." If someone thinks that using a high, squeaky voice is what is meant by "singing," you could tell him: "Sing your story again, using a lower voice." Say the opposite to the child who sings too low. To the person who speaks and forgets to sing say: "Don't forget to use your singing voice."

Other cautions you might need include: "Try again, and see if you can make the music come to an end," "Hold some words a little longer," or "Sing your story faster." Many children will want at least two chances to make the music the way they want it.

Some children may be reluctant to take a turn. Sometimes this will be because they are not used to hearing their own or others' singing voices, and they are embarrassed. Such feelings usually pass quickly.

But, in some cases, a child does not know what to sing about. If you need to motivate anyone, think of events that have happened or will soon be happening. In September, ask him to sing about what happened during the summer. After birthdays, Christmas or Hanukah, ask children to sing about gifts received, places visited, etc. "I have a new bike. It is blue and silver," one child will sing. Ask children to bring things that interest them to school. Someone might sing: "This is a robin's nest that fell out of a tree. Last summer we watched the robin family."

Singing a Story   (For Grades 1-3)

To sing a story requires more thought than to sing Show and Tell. A story might be a simple statement of fact. More likely, it will have a plot; something special will happen.

You might suggest on one day that everyone sing a statement about himself, telling his name and address or some other statement of fact. "My name is Rita Clark and I live on Harris Street." "Today is Monday. The sun is shining, but it is cold." "I have a sister named Libby. She is in fifth grade."

On another day, ask the children to sing statements in time with hand clapping. This should be done lightly in a fast walk rhythm (about two watch ticks to each clap). Children could sing single sentences the first time they try this exercise. They will soon find out that, in cases where a statement has several syllables, they must be fitted in quickly. If there are few syllables, they must be drawn out. "I am Wen-dy Cum-mings" has no complications, but "I am Chris-to-pher Smith" must be sung speedily on the first name and drawn out on the last.

There are various ways to motivate children to sing a story. You could show them a number of pictures in which something is happening and ask each participant to choose a picture about which to create a story. You could take everyone on a walk and have different children sing about what they saw or did.

There will be imaginative children who enjoy making up fairy tales, and they may be asked to sing their stories. Or an invented story may be more realistic, about people and events that seem real.

If anyone has trouble getting started, try reassuring him. If he needs more help, have him talk about his story before he starts. He may still need a few seconds of silent thought at which time he will be deciding such things as where to pitch his voice, how fast to sing the words, whether to use even or uneven rhythm, etc.

If the children have a lot of experience and become proficient at singing stories, challenge them to experiment with the music. In one set of experiments ask everyone to focus on rhythms. The syllables of words that have important meanings could be held longer than others. When there is fast action or excitement in the story, words should be sung quickly. Even rhythms should be used when singing about people or animals walking, about machinery or vehicles moving smoothly, etc. Uneven rhythms would be used when the story is about horses galloping, children skipping, machinery in the process of breaking down, rabbits hopping, etc.

In another set of experiments suggest that the focus be on the rise and fall in pitch. As the emotions of the characters of a story become more intense, the pitch of the tune could rise. If the emotion being expressed is sadness, if happenings are mysterious, etc., the pitch would be lower. When the story is about something large in size, when men's voices are being imitated, the pitch would remain low. But, if the person sung about is small or dainty, if emotions like fear or great joy are being described, the pitch would remain high.

Children improvising music for a story can create other dramatic effects with their voices. Important words can be accented; the voice can be alternately softened and made loud—to suit the subject. Sometimes a long pause, followed by rapid singing, is an effective way to show excitement.

If they do not do it automatically, coach children to pause at the ends of phrases. Their tunes should evolve around one tone, and the song should usually end on that tone. Let them have time to organize what they are doing so that they will feel satisfied that what they have sung is what they intended.

Other Informal Improvisations   (For Grades 1-6)

If you are a person who can improvise, who can sing what you want to say, try initiating conversations that are sung. You could choose a moment of the day when routine has made everyone weary or when there are sounds of confusion as a lot of children are chatting.

You can invent verbal exchanges. For example, without announcing what you intend to do, sing: "Will ev'ryone who's wearing blue today—please stand." ..... "Kenneth, what part of you is blue?" ..... "Sally, what blue thing do you have on?" .....

Improvised songs can be used to study many subjects. You can encourage the children to sing their answers in sentences. If the subject is mathematics, you could start: "John, please tell me, how much is three plus nine?" ..... "Debbie, I ask you, if you take six from six, how much have you left?" ..... The children could play this game by themselves. Social studies, spelling, science facts—these are some of the subjects that can be studied.

To dismiss children for recess, lunch, or home, try singing. You start, after which the person named is the next singer. You might sing: "I excuse Diana and her row (or group); whom does Diana excuse?" She might respond with: "I excuse Andrew and his row. Andrew, whom do you excuse?" Each child named takes a turn until everyone has left.

You could ask older children to invent new products and try to sell them by means of amusing commercials. Advertisements like "Shine-O Trumpet Polish will keep your trumpets shiney," "Uncle Wilbur's Wild and Wonderful Wheat Germ Waffles," or "Our Gummy Gooey Glue is guaranteed the gooiest!" can be sung with improvised tunes.

Singing a Short Poem   (For Grades 1-3)

The children either may find a short poem—two to four lines long—or write their own. You should write the words on the chalk board and ask the children to read them together. After you have made sure everyone can read all words, all words are understood, and the meaning of the poem is clear, have the poem read with appropriate expression—with pauses, words drawn out or stressed, high pitch on some, low on others, and so on. For example:

> 1. To keep busy while they're sitting,
>   Ladies talk and do their knitting.

> 2. There was a boy who wasn't nice;
>   He ate a giant bowl of rice—twice!

Show the children how to scan the words in rhythm, stressing important syllables and taking care not to accent the less important syllables. Have individual children scan the poem.

When preliminaries have been completed, tell the children to get ready to sing the poem. They should go over the words twice to themselves. The first time they are to think the words; the second time, they are to imagine they are singing them. As soon as someone is ready to sing aloud, he should raise his hand.

More periods of silence may be needed as the children take turns singing the poem. A tune that someone has thought of can be forgotten while someone else is singing his tune, and time should be allowed to let each person recover his own tune.

Singing a Longer Poem   (For Grades 4-6)

A longer poem can be found, can be written by someone in the class, or can be written as a class project. The children should have more than one to choose from, unless the class writes one together. The words should be written on the board, and lines or phrases should be written one under the other.

Backward, Inside Out and Upside Down

> 1. Would you like to eat your dinner
>   In the morning, half-past nine?
>   Break fast in the afternoon
>   And eat your lunch when stars do shine?

> *Chorus:* Oh, my friend, you've got things backward,
>   Inside out and upside down;
>   If folks did as you suggested,
>   That would turn the world around!

> 2. Would you like to drive your auto
>   Far across the ocean wide?
>   Come back home in time for Christmas,
>   Rolling in at low high tide?

> *Chorus . . . . .*

Have the class read the words together. Make sure everyone can read all the words, that they understand them and get the meaning of the poem. In the poem above, one person or group can read the verses, another speak the chorus. Ask the class to scan the words, accenting strong syllables and dropping voices on the un-accented syllables. Usually a group knows automatically how to scan, but, if there are problems, have everyone clap lightly while saying the words.

If the poem chosen has a chorus, ask the children to make up a tune for it which can be memorized and sung after each verse. Then have different individuals sing the verses. They should try to create tunes that lead into the music of the chorus.

Another method of creating music for a longer poem is to have as many children sing it as there are phrases. A different child is assigned to each phrase.

The most important part of the song is the music of the first phrase. The person who sings it sets the character of the song. He establishes the tempo, the rhythm pattern, the key around which the tones pivot (and the key note on which the song will end), and perhaps a note pattern. The music of the first phrase will sound unfinished, as if a question is being asked, and the singer of the second phrase must make up music that seems to answer the question of the first. It often happens that the music of the third phrase of a song will be exactly the same as or very similar to that of the first. It will have a questioning tone which will be "answered," brought to a close, by the fourth singer.

If they request it, the first group of composers should be given another chance, to see if they can improve on their first attempt. Other groups may then take turns composing music for the same poem. The class should discuss the merits of the various attempts, and choose the music they like best. This could be sung enough times so that everyone can learn it. Or, the song could be recorded on the tape recorder. Then, if there is more than one stanza, the music can be used to sing the other words.

PREPARATION FOR WRITING SONGS   (FOR GRADES 2-6)

If your children tried any of the exercises in improvisation, they were not asked to pay strict attention to the components of the music. They will have discovered, without having it pointed out, that there is an underlying and regular beat when music is composed for a poem that has rhythm. And if the poem has an even number of phrases, the singers who improvise music for it will probably have automatically composed phrases that seemed to alternately ask questions and give answers.

In the exercises below you will lead your children to recognize and use the question-and-answer aspect of phrases of music. Words are suggested to help you present the lessons. You can use your discretion about motivating, amplifying, and reviewing these lessons as needed.

Recognizing Question-and-Answer Phrases in Music

Children should have music books at hand.

"A sentence in music is called a phrase." Write "phrase" on the chalkboard. "In a song, the words are in word phrases, and the notes are in music phrases, and usually these phrases are together. They last for the same amount of time. We know when a word phrase begins in a song because the first word begins with a capital letter. Also, these word phrases often rhyme at the end. What do we call a set of rhyming phrases?" (We call it a poem.)

"Find a song in your books that everyone knows and likes, and raise your hand as soon as you know the page number." ..... "I would like someone to read the first phrase of the poem and stop." ..... "Someone read the words of the second phrase and stop." ..... "I am going to divide you into two groups" ..... "and you will take turns singing the phrases of the song. Group One will sing the first phrase, Group Two the second, Group One the third, and so on." .....

"Now I would like Group One to sing alone. Every time they come to a phrase belonging to Group Two, they should think it without making a sound. Everyone in Group One should try to start together on their phrases." .....

"How did the music of these phrases make you feel?" If the children failed to notice, ask everyone to hum the music of the first phrase and stop. They should remark that stopping there makes them feel uncomfortable, that it sounds unfinished, etc.

"The first phrase of every group of two makes people feel uncomfortable. It is as if the music is asking a question. Let's have Group One sing the first phrase and Group Two sing the second and stop. You should listen to the music and decide if you think the second phrase 'answers' the 'question' of the first." ..... If the music of the second phrase of the song chosen happens to only partially "answer" the music of the first, tell the children to sing the next two phrases and as many sets of phrases as necessary to get the "final" answer.

"So that we can hear better how the phrases of music seem to ask questions and give answers, I would like you to sing the tune of our song without words. Sing every note with the syllable 'la' (or "loo" or any neutral syllable you prefer). The groups should take turns as before. Group One starts." .....

"What do we call a sentence in music?" (It is called a phrase.) "In a set of two musical phrases, which phrase sounds as if it is asking a question?" (The first phrase questions.) "How does the music of the second phrase of the pair sound?" (It sounds as if it is answering the question of the first phrase.)

On another day, have a follow-up or review lesson. Use the same procedure, or try the following. Find a recording of a song that is slow in tempo. Ask the children to raise their hands at the end of the first phrase—at the "question mark." Start the record again and have them show that they recognize phrases by counting how many sets of "questions" and "answers" they have heard. (Some children might find it easier to count the total number of phrases they hear.)

Speaking Question-and-Answer Phrases in Rhythm

All the rhythms of music can be resolved into an even one-two, one-two, the rhythm of the walk. In walking we step first on one foot, then the other, back and forth, left-right, left-right. If you speed up a waltz in 3/4 time or a skip or gallop in 6/8 meter, you will discover a steady one-two, one-two rhythm,

These steady rhythms are also found in the chants of young people—nursery rhymes, counting rhymes, cheerleader yells, words for ball-bouncing, jump-rope, clapping games and other playground activities. "One, two, buckle my shoe ....." "One, two, three O'Leary ....." "Jack and Jill went up the hill ....." "Two, four, six, eight; Who do we ap-pre-ci-ate? ....." The tap of a ball or jump-rope on the ground indicates the rhythm for some chants. But more often, they are spoken without such mechanical aids. One can guess that such natural functions as walking and breathing or having one's heart beat give people a natural inclination to feel a steady beat underlying chants, poetry and music.

Our conversational speech lacks this kind of even rhythm. In the following exercise, children will need a means of keeping a steady beat. Suggest that they use "body instruments." They might discover what they can do to make sound with parts of their bodies—clap hands, snap fingers, tap shoulders, tap toes, stamp feet, patch (slap thighs), etc. These can be combined. For example, the children could alternately slap thighs and snap fingers or slap desks and clap hands, etc.

Explain to the class that while a beat is being kept, you will be asking questions of different individuals. The child who is questioned must answer in the rhythm of the beating. Warn that they will need to speak some words quickly to get them in in time; others will need to be held or spoken slowly. At other times it may be necessary to wait a moment before speaking. The following examples will illustrate the kinds of accommodations it may be necessary to make.

Example 1. There is an even number of syllables. No accommodation is needed.

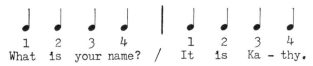

```
  1    2    3    4   |   1    2    3    4
What  is  your name? /  It   is  Ka - thy.
```

Example 2. Some syllables must be spoken faster.

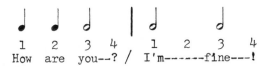

```
  1    2    3      4   |  1    2      3    4
When  is  Jan-u---a--ry? / Af - ter De - cem-ber.
```

Example 3. Some words must be held.

```
  1    2    3   4  |  1    2    3    4
How  are  you--? / I'm------fine---!
```

Example 4. Pauses are used to keep the rhythm.

```
  1      2    3    4  |  1   2      3    4
Do you have sis-ters? / ----No,  I   don't--.
```

(Note: In the above examples, music notation has been used; a number appears for every beat for the benefit of those who do not know the time value of note symbols.)

The above questions and answers can be spoken in other rhythms. Following are the same words and other possibilities.

Example 1.

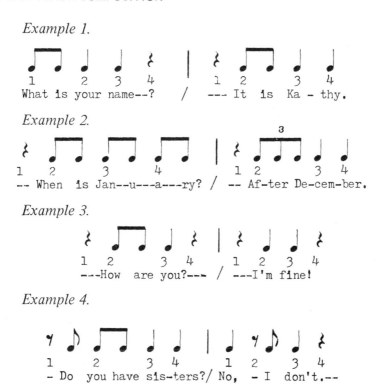

Example 2.

Example 3.

Example 4.

When children are creating, they should be discouraged from imitating what others have done. Tell them that any rhythm is acceptable, as long as it fits with the basic beat.

If you are doing this exercise with young children, plan to ask the same question of several of them. Older children will enjoy the challenge of a variety of questions that force them to think and stay alert.

Choose a method of keeping the beat. Clap, snap, slap, tap, use body instruments, tap pencils on desks, etc. You may want to divide the class into small groups which will take turns keeping the beat. The beat should proceed at a walk rate (two to three ticks of a watch for each beat). While you are asking a question, point to (or nod to) the person who is to respond. Possible questions and responses for young children might be:

"What is your name?" "My name is ....."
"How old are you?" "I am ..... years old."
"Do you have brothers (sisters)?" "(Yes, No), I (do, don't)."

Questions and answers for older children might include:

"Where do you live?" "I live on ..... Street."

"What month is this?" "This is ....."

"What is today's date?" "Today is ....."

"What date is Christmas?" "December twenty-fifth"

"Where is Canada?" "North of the U.S.A." ("In North America," etc.)

"What sport do you like?" "I like ....."

"Tell me your hobby." "My hobby's ....." ("I have no hobby.")

The same individual can be asked a two-part question:

"Do you like ice cream?" ..... "Which flavor do you like?"

"Do you like stories?" ..... "Have you a fav'rite?"

"What is your fav'rite store?" ..... "What do you like to buy?"

Turn the activity over to the children. They should think of short questions that require short answers, and these can be written on the chalk board. "What color are your eyes?" and "Have you a fav'rite song?" are examples of questions they could use.

This activity can be used to study mathematics. Put ten or more easy problems on the board. Choose a child to ask the question, and ask all the children to keep the beat. A younger child might ask: "How much is three plus four?" and indicate who is to answer. The person who answers should make a complete sentence: "Three plus four is seven." It would then be his turn to ask the next question.

Problems for older children can be a little harder. Include easy multiplication and division, as well as addition and subtraction. Longer problems can be challenging: "Start with six and add sixteen; subtract twenty-one. What is left?"

Ask the children to discuss the activity. What did the speaker do if he had many syllables to speak while the beat was being kept? What kind of adjustment did a speaker have to make when there were only a few syllables to be spoken?

Singing Question-and-Answer Phrases in Rhythm

Once your children have had experience in speaking questions and answers in rhythm, they should be able to plan the words they will use and at the same time make up tunes for them.

The improvisations suggested at the beginning of the chapter were informal exercises. In this exercise the singer must use phrases, and he must sing them in strict rhythm.

You can use the same procedure for singing question-and-answer phrases as in the exercise for speaking them. You could start the activity by singing a question to someone without announcing what you plan to do. Not only should the words ask a question; the music of the phrase should sound unfinished or questioning. The words and music of the answer should both bring matters to a close.

An exercise like this can be enjoyable and challenging. It may seem like a game, and you and the children could carry it on at different times during the day.

WRITING MUSICAL NOTATION   (FOR GRADES 2-6)

A child learns music in much the same way as he learns speech. Before he can speak words, he must hear them spoken. He imitates the speech of others; then he figures out how to use words of his own invention to communicate with people. Eventually, he is introduced to the word symbols that represent the words he hears and speaks. Finally, he is taught the letters that stand for the sounds in the words, and he learns to write them. Then he can communicate by writing the words he knows how to speak.

The child can go through a similar procedure with music. He hears the songs of others and sings them by imitation. He creates his own songs. He learns to read the note symbols that stand for the sounds of the songs. Finally, he learns to write the notes that stand for the sounds in the songs.

A note of music must tell the reader two things—how much time he should give it and how low or high he should pitch it in relation to the notes around it. Because of the double meaning in each music note, writing music is considered complicated.

To simplify the task of teaching students to write notes, we will suggest words for you to use. Only three kinds of notes will be presented, those that proceed at the three rates of speed most commonly used in songs—a walk rate, a slow walk rate which is twice as slow as walk rate, and a fast rate that we will call "run" because it goes twice as fast as the walk rate. The terms "quarter," "half," and "eighth" note will not be introduced. The walk (quarter) note will be considered to be the basic beat.

The more difficult task in music writing is to indicate the pitch of the notes the composer wishes to use. In word writing a person can use a knowledge of phonics to figure out how to spell the words he wants to use. In music writing a person could hunt for his melody using trial and error on a tuned instrument like the piano. But there is another dependable method which a composer, experienced or not, can use to figure out the pitch of notes. If he knows the music scale, this gives him a "key." In the lessons below, we will use the Latin "so-fa" syllables. The letter names—C D E F G A B C—will not be used.

To further reduce the possibility of your having problems, we recommend that you use the C scale only. This is the only scale that has no sharps or flats; in other words, it can be played on the piano, using only the white keys. The chief reason for using a scale that would start on a note other than C is to accommodate the voices of singers. People with higher-pitched voices are not comfortable when asked to sing using notes that are suited for people with naturally lower voices, and vice versa. Whenever the tones of a song in the scale of C are moved higher or lower to accommodate a singer's voice, sharps or flats must be used, and this complicates the music writer's job.

Whether a composer is experienced or not in writing music, getting the notes of a song onto paper takes time. In this section you will find out how to teach your children to record music, using the system of putting notes on staff lines, the system which is generally used in western countries and most areas of the world.

Picturing Rhythm with Notes and Rests

"People had been singing and making up music for thousands of years. Finally, they realized that they needed a way of writing their music to show how fast it was to go. Like the music of today, some of it moved quickly. At other times it went more slowly, and there were times when it went very very slowly. Someone noticed that most of the music seemed to 'walk' right along, about as fast as voices move along when people are talking to each other. The inventors of music notes tried several different marks and little pictures of 'o's. As you know, every song and every piece of music has several places where the music 'walks' along. The note for walk speed had to be small and easy to draw. Here is how they finally decided to make it." Use the side of a piece of chalk about an inch long. Make a single short stroke by moving the chalk diagonally from upper right to lower left. This is the note "head." To its right, approximately three inches above the head, draw a vertical line, the "stem," to connect with the right side of the head. ♩ (Do not have the children learn the name, quarter note, at this time.)

"Notice that the head of the note is filled in. In music books these notes are black. The black color of the note head reminds us of the head of a person whose hair has not yet turned grey or white from age. He can walk right along when he is going somewhere. This note can be called a 'walk' note.

"Everyone clap four walk notes and stop. Go this fast—one, two, ready, clap." ..... "Halfway down the chalkboard I would like four people to make those four walk notes. They should be in a straight row, fairly close together. Use short pieces of chalk about an inch long, and make a short stroke for the head the way I just did. The line of the stem should come straight down to the head." ..... "Everyone clap the walk notes on the board while I point to them. One, two, ready, clap." .....

"The picture of a note that moves twice as slow as the walk notes we have just made and clapped is the same shape as a walk note, but it is not filled in." Draw a "slow walk" note by making the oval head first and adding the stem after. ♩ "A note like this appears to represent an older person with white hair who walks twice as slow as a person with dark hair. I would like two people to draw two 'slow walk' notes in a straight line under the four walk notes. They should make the note head first and add the stem after." .....

"I would like everyone to clap the notes on the board and say the names as we clap. Stay with me. I will point to the notes in order. When you come to the 'slow walk' notes, clap only on the word 'slow' and hold your hands together on the word 'walk.' One, two, ready, go." .....

Older children may continue the lesson. If you stop here, you should review the work with walk and slow notes before going on to the next part.

"We have discovered the notes that people invented years ago to show two rates of speed. There are others. Can you guess what some of them might be?" ..... Children's answers might include uneven rhythms like skips. Someone will probably name fast notes.

"It is important to know how to show the fast notes in music. The ones that go about as fast as people run look exactly like walk notes, except that there is a flag at the top of the stem. This might remind you of a scarf that is waving in the breeze as the note runs." ♪ When you draw a "run" note, make the head, the stem, and the flag in that order.

The following poem can be recited to give young children a feeling of the speed and appearance of the run note. When you recite it, give each word or syllable the same amount of time, stopping only at the end. Make your voice move along quickly.

The Run Note

> Look! There goes the little note
> Who wears a scarf a-round his throat;
> He runs to keep it in the air;
> He's always running ev'rywhere.

"I would like eight people to draw eight run notes on the chalk board above the four walk notes. Make them close together, about three inches apart. They should be made like walk notes. At the end, put a flag on top of the stem of each note." .....

"I am going to point to the rows of notes on the board, and as I point to each note, I would like everyone to say the note's name and clap how fast it goes. One, two, ready, go. Run run run run run, etc." ..... After you have proceeded from row to row in order, move, unannounced, to different rows, the same row, etc.

"The writers of music notes discovered long ago that it took them a long time to make the flags on every little run note. When they were in a hurry, they would make two flags with one stroke of the pen. It was as if there was an invisible knot. Watch." Erase one flag of a pair of run notes on the board and draw a short horizontal line extending toward the second note. ♩ Then, erase the flag of the second note and make a short line that meets the line of the first note. ♩ Quickly make another set of run notes, showing how easily the bar can be made at the top. ♫

On another day have the children review the three kinds of notes they have learned. Everyone should have a turn at drawing them. Then have them learn to make the same notes upside down. The children may have music books at hand for reference.

"The three kinds of notes which we have learned to draw have had their heads at the bottom and their stems straight up on the right side. If you look on almost any page of any music book, you will notice that the same notes—walk, slow walk, and run—are sometimes made upside down. Can anyone figure out why this should be?" ..... If no one has an idea, you could say:

"Suppose a note on the top line or space of a music staff had a stem going up. Can you imagine what would happen?" (The stem might run into the words of the line of music above the staff of the note.) "To keep stems from getting in the way of other lines of music, we must make those for notes above the middle line of the staff to drop down, and those for notes below the middle line to go up. The note head is the same; the stem is on the left. If you look at the same notes when your music books are upside down, you will see where the stem goes. The notes are the same, in the way that you would be the same person even if you were standing on your head.

"I would like three people to make pictures on the board of the three kinds of notes we know turned upside down." Selected children make ♭ ♭ and ♭ .

Draw a staff of five lines on the board. Use a staff liner, a holder for five pieces of chalk, evenly spaced. If none is available, you can draw the lines free-hand. The quickest way is to make two parallel lines at a time. Take two pieces of chalk. Hold one as you would a pencil and the other between the next two fingers (the middle and ring fingers). The thumb must hold both pieces of chalk securely. You can then draw both chalks straight across the board.

Make note heads in various places on the staff, some high, some in the middle, some down low. Choose children to add stems, making them go in the proper directions.

"We have been learning to picture music notes, but there are times when a person is writing music that he wants no sound. Does anyone know the name of the music symbol for silence?" (It is called a rest.) "If the silence is to last as long as a walk note, the rest is a wiggly line, like this: ⋚ . Watch while I make a walk rest slowly, and count how many parts there are to the line." (There are four parts.) "Try making a walk rest in the air with the pointer finger of the hand you write with. Stay with my voice. Down right, down left, down right, and hook." The children should practice making this in the air a few times.

"Put the same finger on your desk (or book cover), and try making the walk rest a little faster. Down, down, down, hook." Have the children make a few more. "The people I choose may make four walk rests each on the chalk board." .....

"Other kinds of rests are easier to make. To draw a rest that lasts only as long as a run note, think of the number seven. Give it a fancy top, like this. ❼ Each of the children I choose can make four run rests on the chalk board." .....

"Another rest that is easy to draw is the one that lasts as long as a slow walk note. It looks like a small black hat with a straight brim— ▄▄ . Will the people I choose please come to the chalk board and make four slow walk rests each." ..... Urge children to write music symbols as quickly as possible.

Writing Rhythm Dictation

To give children practice in writing the notes they hear, have them write what you dictate (by clapping) on plain paper. Some children may write on the chalk board.

The examples of notes that can be dictated are divided into three sections and range from easy to difficult. Children of all ages should start with the easy exercises. The youngest should continue with easy dictation only. Older children may eventually be able to work up to the difficult exercises.

Notes should be clapped. Rests should be indicated by holding hands apart, palms upward.

A good sequence is: 1. You clap the exercise. 2. The children clap it after you. 3. The children clap it again and say the notes (or rests) they have heard. 4. They write on the board or on paper. 5. You clap one more time, and they check their work.

Writing Rhythm Notation for a Poem

Choose a short poem like one of the following, and write it on the chalk board at a height where children can reach. Divide words into syllables for young children only. Leave space between each line.

1. Trains go speed-ing on the track;
   Click-ty clack, click-ty clack.

2. The wind is strong; it blows so hard;
   It blows the leaves in-to our yard.

3. "Hi, Mom! What's for lunch?"
   "Hot dogs and or-ange punch."

4. Go to Eng-land, go to Spain;
   See the cas-tles in the rain.
   Go to Hol-land, go to France;
   See the hap-py peo-ple dance.

"Today we are going to discover the note rhythm of the poem on the board. Let's read the words together. Ready, go." ..... "Will someone please read the poem alone?" ..... "Can anyone find words that are hard to read? Are there any words you do not understand?" ..... "Let's read it together once more." .....

If words are not divided into syllables, say: "Do you see any words that have more than one syllable?" ..... "I would like someone to come to the board and make hyphens between syllables." .....

"When we read the poem this time, we will be clapping even beats. We must keep our voices with the claps. Clap with me ..... Read the words with me .....

"This time when we clap and say the words, we will accent the first of every two claps, so that the clapping sounds loud, soft, loud, soft. One, two, ready, go ..... And stop.

"Now I would like someone to go to the board. We will read and clap the poem again, and when the person at the board hears an accented syllable, he should make a short vertical stroke over that syllable, like this: /." In the first poem above, for example, accented syllables would be indicated as follows:

> Trains go speed-ing on the track;
> Click-ty clack, click-ty clack.

"I would like someone else to go to the board and mark the syllables that are unaccented and spoken softly with an upside-down eyebrow, like this: / . The person must listen carefully for every soft clap and put a mark at the exact place at which it happens. Sometimes the same word or syllable will have both an accent mark and the mark of no accent. We will clap and say the words as before. Clap first ..... Ready to read ..... "

In the example we are using, the words "track," "clack," and "clack" will have two claps each, one accented, the other unaccented. These should be indicated thus:

Trains go speed-ing on the track;
Click-ty clack, click-ty clack.

"Will everyone please check the poem to see if we have left any syllables unmarked. If there are any, we must put an unaccented syllable mark over each one." The sample poem has none.

"Music writers put accented and unaccented syllables together in groups. The accented syllable comes first, and it is followed by as many unaccented syllables as come after. To show the end of a group of syllables, a music writer makes a short line straight up and down. Such a line is called a measure bar. At the very end of the music, he makes a double bar. In the poem on the board, where should we place the first measure bar? Remember that it must come just after the unaccented syllable in the first group; this will be just before the next accented syllable." ..... Draw the first measure bar yourself to show the children how to do it. Invite different people to put in succeeding measure bars. Be sure to include those at the ends of lines. There will be none at the beginning of a line. There should be a double bar at the end.

Trains go | speed-ing | on the | track; |

Click-ty | clack, | click-ty | clack. ||

"Some of the words and syllables of our poem have been spoken about as fast as people walk. Let's say our poem without clapping and listen for the syllables that are spoken in walk note rhythm." ..... "I would like someone to go to the chalk board and make the head of a walk note over each of those words as we say the poem. Make a quick stroke with the side of a short piece of chalk." ..... "The person at the board should put stems on the heads." .....

"Say the poem to yourselves in rhythm, and decide if any syllables are held as long as a slow walk note." ..... In the poem we have been using, the words "track," "clack," and "clack" are held. I would like someone to go to the board and draw a slow walk note over each of these syllables or words." .....

"Go over the poem to yourselves one more time to find out if any syllables were spoken in run note rhythm." ..... In the sample poem used here there is no run note rhythm.

"We have written music notes over words and syllables of our poem. Why is it a good idea to write notes that tell how fast to go?" (Other people who know what the notes mean can look at what we have written and know exactly how fast we wanted the words to be read. Also, having the notes will help us remember how we planned the rhythm today; in time, we might forget.)

Other rhythm arrangements are possible for the same poem. Older or more capable students might enjoy discovering some of these. The poem we have used might be spoken in this rhythm:

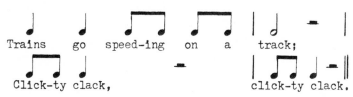

Learning Scale Names

If the children are already familiar with the Latin or so-fa syllables, the following study may be omitted. Do not teach them the letter names of notes at this time.

"Long ago, when people were inventing music writing, they had to think of a way to tell other people how high or how low a tune was to go. They soon realized that for most of the music they were composing, they were using the same notes over and over. It is like the way we use the same letters over and over in different words. However, when they counted the different notes, they discovered that they made only seven different sounds. There were other notes that sounded similar, except they sounded high, and some sounded similar, except that they were lower; but still there were only seven different ones. They finally decided to name each note by using the first syllable of seven words in an old Latin church song—do re mi fa so la and ti. Does anyone know what we now call this group of notes in music?" (It is called a scale.)

"I would like everyone who knows the scale to sing it. Please sing just slowly enough so that I can write the names on the chalk board as you sing. When you get to the last note, high do, sing it again and continue singing down the scale." Give the pitch, low C, or hum a low tone. Start writing at a low point on the far left side of the board. Move gradually higher, placing each note as if it was located on an ascending step of an invisible staircase. Write the descending scale on descending "steps."

"If we know the music scale, we can use it to figure out the notes of the tunes we might create. Today we will try to memorize the seven notes. Sing up and down the scale while I point to each

note." ..... "Now, I shall erase one of the names in both scales .....
Sing the scale again, filling in the missing names." ..... "Once again, I
shall erase a name from both scales ..... Can you still sing all the notes
of the scale?" .....

Continue to erase note names. The children should sing after
each erasure until they can sing the entire scale by memory.

Review the scale names on other occasions, until the children
know them thoroughly. One way to vary the review procedure is to
force everyone to recall the full name of each syllable by writing
only the first letter of each on the board as a reminder. "D" would
represent "do," "r" represent "re," etc.

Encourage the children to practice the scale at odd moments
of the day. It can become part of your opening exercises; it can be
sung while everyone is putting on coats for recess or while walking
out to recess or to go home, etc. You can start the singing, and
expect everyone to join in.

Picturing the Notes of the Scale on a Staff of Lines

"Long ago, after people had given names to the seven notes
of the music scale, they had to think of a way to picture them in
writing. They had to show that the first note sounds low and that the
notes gradually get higher. Finally they decided to use a set of lines,
and nowadays, music writers still write notes on a set of lines. Does
anyone know what the lines are called?" (They are called a staff.)
"Does anyone know how many lines there are in a modern staff?"
(There are five lines.)

Draw a short staff on the chalk board:

"As soon as the music writers had drawn the five lines, they
realized that they could make notes, not only on the lines, but also
in the spaces between the lines. How many spaces are there?" (There
are four spaces.)

Draw at least four open note heads in succession on the lines
and spaces of your staff:

"Even though they had five lines and four spaces, music
writers still did not have places to put the very highest and the very
lowest-sounding notes of their compositions. Do you know or can
you guess what they did to show those notes?" Someone may point
out that they made other staffs. Music for the piano is written on

two staffs. Higher-pitched instruments like the violin and trumpet have music written on the upper staff; instruments like the 'cello or trombone use the lower staff.

Another way music writers solved the problem of having places to put the lowest-sounding (or highest-sounding) notes was to draw short lines below the staff (or above it). Show how this is done by adding one or more ledger lines below and above the lines of your staff on the chalk board: ⸺

"A tune in music can move in three possible directions. It might move up to higher notes, or it might go down to lower notes. Can anyone tell me the third possible direction?" (The third direction could be described as straight across; the tune stays in one place with the same note being sounded more than once.)

"Today we will write the scale we have been singing on a staff of lines." Draw a staff approximately three feet long on the board. "To show that the notes we will write should be sounded by people with voices as high as yours (not as low as men's voices), we must make a G clef at the beginning of the staff. Notice that it looks like a fancy capital G with a curl around the second line of the staff." At the left edge of your staff, draw a straight vertical line from just above to just below the lines. Return to the top and loop right, as if to make letter "P." Without removing the chalk, continue downward, making a capital "G" whose end curls around the G line, the second line of the staff.

"When we start singing the scale, our voices are at their lowest. Therefore, we will need a short line below the staff on which to write the first note." Make a ledger line to the right of your G clef. "I would like someone to draw an open note head for 'do' on this line. Do not color it in or put a stem on it for now." In this exercise the children will be learning to picture pitch without rhythm.

"The person who makes 're' should put it to the right of 'do.' A space should be left between the two notes about as wide as the space for another note." You could make a phantom note. "Re" should touch the edge of your note:

"I would like the next person to write both 'mi' and 'fa.' " Having one child make two successive notes will give him experience in writing both on a line and in a space. The rest of the class will benefit from watching. "Who can write the last four notes of the scale moving upward?" .....

Choose any number of children to write the descending scale.

"I would like everyone to sing the music from the staff while I point to the notes." ..... "Will someone else please point to the notes that we have just written. Everyone sing again." .....

Writing Notes in Other Scale Sequences

The tunes of songs often go back and forth on the notes of the scale; sometimes the same note is sounded over and over. It is not necessary to make skips to create an interesting and respectable tune. Of the twenty-five notes in "Mary Had a Little Lamb," all but one go stepwise or are repeated, and that one makes a modest skip, jumping over only one other note. The famous Chorale melody in Beethoven's ninth symphony has no skips whatsoever for the first eight measures, a total of thirty notes.

When a tune has wide skips, it can be difficult to figure out the notes. A song like "The Star Spangled Banner," for instance, begins by skipping back and forth on the notes of the tonic chord and would be very hard to figure out. But, in the song, "America," the notes mostly go up or down the scale a step at a time, or a single note is repeated. There are just four skips in a total of forty-one notes, and these are easy to figure out.

With the following exercise you will be preparing your children to write tunes in other scale sequences than straight up or down. Make a long staff on the chalk board. Add a G clef. Sing or say the notes of the following.

"Who can come to the board and write 'do, do, do?' " ..... "Can someone write 'do re do?' " ..... "Who could write 'do re mi do?' " ..... "I would like someone to write 'mi mi fa fa mi.' "

Continue dictation, using repeated notes or short groups of notes in scale sequence only. Try to use each note at least once. Do not skip notes unless to return to a recently sung note, as in "do re mi do." Younger children will need the most practice.

Identifying and Writing Notes from the Way They Sound

"Today I am going to sing short tunes for you without telling you the names of the notes. I shall tell you the name of the first note only. After I have sung a tune, think what the notes would be, and raise your hand to tell us." If you prefer not to sing the tunes, play them on the piano. If you sing, use a neutral syllable, like "la," "li" or "loo."

To avoid having to tell the children the name of every starting note, start each new segment on the last note of the previous segment. A possible sequence of tunes might be: do re do, do re mi mi mi, mi fa so la so, so fa mi, mi fa so so so, so la ti do, do ti do ti do, etc.

After your children have shown that they can identify notes from hearing them, they should be able to write them. Draw a long staff on the board. Instruct the children to hear the tune and think what the notes are. When they are ready, they should write them. If necessary, sing or play each tune two or more times.

This exercise can be turned over to older children. Make sure they know the rules: that they make sure everyone knows the beginning note; that notes used must go in order up or down the scale or must be repeated; that they sing tunes on a neutral syllable; that there be no more than five notes in a tune.

Identifying First Notes

How is it possible to figure out the first note of a tune? The secret is in knowing that most tunes begin on one of three different notes—do, mi or so. Out of curiosity I checked a book of one hundred and twenty songs and found that one hundred sixteen of them began on one of those three notes, the notes of the major tonic chord—do, mi, so (or high do). Since it takes little time to try each of these notes in turn, finding the first note of a song need not be a major problem.

Suppose, for example, you wanted to know the first note of "Mary Had a Little Lamb." First, hum the tune to determine in which direction it starts out. In this case, you will find that it proceeds down the scale. Therefore you know that the first three notes will be "do ti la, " "so fa mi," or "mi re do." Sing "do ti la" and remember the tune. Sing "Ma-ry had," using the do-ti-la tune. It should not sound right. Next, test "so fa mi" in the same way. Sing the notes; then sing the words. That will not sound right either. But, when you sing "mi re do" and use those notes for the words, you should notice that the notes and the song sound alike. The first note of the song is "mi."

Identifying a Skip in Notes

It is rare that a tune is created that does not have at least one skip. It was noted above that the skip that occurs when a tune returns to a recently sung note is easy to identify. In a group of notes like "do re mi do," it will be easy to recognize the skip from "mi" to "do" because the first "do" is remembered.

The experienced musician must work at figuring out tonal skips in much the same way as the beginner—by making a "scale check." This somewhat resembles the process a lot of people use when they are looking for something in an alphabetized book. The person searching for the "v" section, for instance, might recite to himself a few letters he knows are near "v," like "t u v w." He then knows he must look after "u" and before "w."

The person who knows the music scale can figure out any interval by singing all the notes from the first interval tone to the second. The beginning music writer should sing the notes out loud. The expert does this silently, or, if the interval is familiar, he knows it by memory and can name it with authority.

To teach children to find the notes of an interval, a procedure like the following is suggested. The song used should be familiar to everyone. No books should be used. For example:

"Sing 'Oh, Susanna' without your books." ..... "Now we are going to sing the tune of the song on the syllable 'la' so that we can hear how it goes up and down the scale. We may also hear places where the notes stay in one place for a while. In other places you may hear the tune skip instead of going by steps of the scale. Be listening while you sing." .....

"We are going to start to sing 'Oh, Susanna' again, and this time you will have a chance to show that you hear when the tune makes a skip. As soon as you hear the first skip, raise your hands and stop singing." ..... The children should sing on "la" the tune of the words "I came from" and stop. "Now, sing the words of the passage and decide which are the words of the skip." (The words are "came from.")

"The first note of the song is 'do.' In what direction do the beginning notes go—up the scale or down it?" (They go up.) "I think that you could sing the notes for 'I came,' but you might not be sure of the next note, the note of the skip. Can anyone figure out how we might recognize that note?" (We could sing up the scale until we heard the note.)

"We must keep the sound of the note we want to recognize in the back of our minds and sing up the scale until we come to it. Sing the notes from the beginning of the song." Help the children, if they need it. They should sing the first three notes, "do re mi," after which they will continue up the scale until they hear the note for "from." This is the note, "so."

"Who heard the note for 'from?' " (It was "so.") "Sing the words, 'I came from,' and, without stopping, sing the notes for those words." .....

At first the children will need to sing out loud all notes from the beginning to the end of an interval to discover what they are. When you think they are ready, ask them to think to themselves up or down the scale when they need to know an interval. The first note of an unknown interval is usually known, and it is only the second note that must be discovered.

WRITING A SONG   (FOR GRADES 2-6)

Preliminary study is necessary before children should be expected to write their own songs. They need to have discovered that music consists of phrases that seem to ask questions and give answers. They need to know how to make the symbols for notes that go at the three rates of speed most often used in music. They should know how to express pitch, using the so-fa syllables. They will then be ready to write their own songs, using a step-by-step procedure like the following.

Step 1: *Write the Poem*

The poem which will be set to music might be one written by one of the children and chosen by the group. Or the class might write one together. A subject can be found in something the children are studying or some experience they have had at school. Is there something special going on that month or at that time of the year? Is there to be a holiday, a school sports event, an assembly with a special theme, or a happening like Book Week?

If the class is writing the poem, encourage brevity. Two lines would be enough for the first attempt of younger children, though it may be easier to express a complete thought in four lines.

Children should have scrap paper and pencil with which to jot down ideas. Start by discussing the topic chosen. If possible, get a title; if no one thinks of a good one, write the topic to one side on the chalkboard. Have everyone think silently of two lines that rhyme and write them on the scrap paper.

After a minute or two, ask those who are ready to recite their two lines. The rest of the class should listen and try to judge which set would be easiest to put to music. Write the words at one side of the chalkboard, leaving the central part of the board for the words and music. If more words are needed, have the children think silently again, and write the words chosen on the board. Ask children to think critically and suggest any changes that are necessary.

Step 2: *Find the Rhythm Pattern of the Words*

Ask older children to divide the words of the poem into syllables; help second- and early-third-grade children to find word divisions if necessary. Put hyphens on the board.

Ask the children to read the poem together. Ask them to chant it, making their voices accent stressed syllables. Send someone to the board. While the class chants the poem again, he should mark accented syllables with short vertical strokes. Someone else can mark unaccented syllables with the upside down eyebrows.

Have the poem read again in the accent pattern, and ask the children if they like it or think it should be changed. (Sometimes the natural way of chanting is too singsong.) Have the old pattern erased if the class agrees on a change, and new accents written in.

When the poem is ready, ask the children to put in measure bars. A measure bar should follow unaccented syllables. A double (measure) bar is placed at the end of the poem.

Next, notes indicating the different rates of speed at which the syllables were spoken must be written over each syllable. Start with finding all the syllables that require notes of one speed—perhaps slow walk, since they are easy to detect. Children may clap at a walk rate if necessary. When they hear two claps for a syllable, that syllable should have a slow walk note written above it. They can then go on to discover all syllables requiring walk notes and finally, those that need run notes.

Step 3: *Prepare the Staff and Write the Words*

When you write a song—whether it is one you are composing or one you are copying—always draw staff lines long enough for a line of poetry first and put in a G clef at the beginning of the staff. On the first line only, leave space to the right of the clef sign in which to write a time signature. The second step is to write the words under the staff lines. Draw as many staffs as needed, one for each line of poetry, and write the words. Put hyphens between syllables, but omit accent marks.

Next, a child may copy the measure bars onto the staff. These should not be put between words and syllables; they belong in the same places, but should be placed above the words in the staffs.

Finally, the time signature should be determined. This is a fraction, and should be written to the right of the first G clef. Ask the children to tell you how many claps they made in each measure. This will be the top number. If the walk note is given a beat, the bottom number should be four, the number of its usual name, quarter note. (In some compositions, other notes are given the beat. If the bottom number is eight, the eighth or run note is the unit of beat. A much slower composition could have two for the bottom number, indicating that the half or slow walk note was the note which was given the beat.)

Step 4. *Create the Tune and Write the Notes*

The procedure for creating a tune is similar to the procedure for improvising described at the beginning of this chapter, except that the composer should plan to stay as much as possible in the scale pattern, moving up and down on scale tones and not allowing the tune to make too many skips.

Sound middle C (on a piano, pitchpipe or other instrument). Tell the children that this is "do," and they should plan to start on do, mi, so or high do. They should think the first line to themselves twice. The first time they would chant it in rhythm. The second time sing it in the rhythm. (You might need to sound "do" again.) As soon as someone is ready to sing it out loud, he should raise his hand.

After the first singer has sung his version of the first line, other volunteers should take turns. If necessary, have the children think the words in rhythm again. Sound "do" every time a new singer is preparing. If many tunes are sung and there is a chance their creators will forget them, have them sung on tape.

After the children have decided on the tune they prefer, have its creator teach it to everyone. A tune should be well memorized so that it can be retrieved easily while it is being written.

Find the first note of the tune by testing. Sing the first few notes of it using scale names, starting with "do" as first note. If this does not sound right, try starting with "mi," and if it still sounds wrong, call the first note "so."

Check the rhythm of the first note, and have someone write it on the board in its proper place on the staff, directly over the first syllable.

Everyone should sing the tune on a neutral syllable like "la," and listen for the direction(s) the tune takes. Sound the first note, and have it sung with notes. If the tune skips (is not in scale steps) have the interval notes figured out. Notes should be sung with syllable names enough times to be memorized.

If possible, have a child write the notes on the staff on the board. Note heads should be written first. These go directly over each word syllable, shaded heads for all run and walk notes, open heads for slow walk notes, rests if there is an absence of sound. A different child can refer to the word text to add stems.

Use the same procedure for the remaining lines of the poem, making sure that each new part of the tune relates to the previous part. Remind the children that the first line may sound questioning and the second have an answering tone, the third line question again, the fourth answer, etc. The last line must sound like the end.

In summary, the steps for succeeding lines of the song would be: 1. Everyone sings the lines that have been written; 2. Each child thinks to himself how he would continue the song; 3. Children are given turns to sing their tunes; 4. The class chooses the tune it likes best and sings it enough times to memorize it; 5. The first note of the line is determined by relating it to the last note of the previous line; the note is written; 6. The tune is sung on a neutral syllable to find the direction of the notes; 7. Notes are sung, using syllable names; 8. A child makes note heads on the staff; 9. Another child makes stems and flags for the notes.

Using this system of music writing, songs can be written in other keys, if accommodation is needed for voices that would be more comfortable in higher or lower positions. Other rhythms can be used like the irregular rhythm in the first few measures of the "Battle Hymn of the Republic" or some of the words in "America, the Beautiful" ("beautiful" and "spacious skies" in the first line). Once the procedure for writing songs has been learned, it is easy to learn to write music of greater complexity.

Alternative Ways of Writing Music   (For Grades 4-6)

The method of writing music with notes on staff lines is used by peoples all over the world. It allows the writer to record exactly what he wants to express in music. But, perhaps because it was worked out by a number of people over a period of many years, it is a far from perfect system.

Suggest to your students that they imagine that a system of recording music had never been invented. Without music staffs, notes as we know them and names for those notes, could they invent a method of recording music that would be effective?

Have the children choose a well known tune, a song everyone knows. Suggest that they might use straight lines, blocks, curved lines, etc. They should try to show the direction of the tune as well as the length of time each tone is to be held. For example, here are three different ways of charting the first two phrases of "Yankee Doodle."

Yan-kee Doo-dle went to town, rid-ing on a po-ny

CREATING SONG PLAYS AND OPERETTAS—
ALL GRADES

Possible ways of creating song plays with children can range from informal improvisations to carefully planned and written operettas. Productions can be for the group only, or they can be for another class, for the whole school or an even larger audience.

Improvising a Song Play

A story in the children's reading books can become a song play. Every child should have a book, and there should be speaking parts as well as narration. Choose a good reader for the narrator and choose as many singers as needed for the characters. Everyone else in the class will be in the chorus.

The narrator reads with his speaking voice. Every time he comes to a quotation, something one of the characters says, he stops. The character, instead of speaking, sings an improvised tune for the quotation. The chorus then sings the last phrase after him, using the tune he has created and changing the pronouns.

For example, if the last phrase contains the pronoun "I," "me," "you," "we," etc. the chorus would change it to "he," "she," "him," "her," "they," "them," etc. For example, in the story of "Jack and the Bean-Stalk," the giant might sing: "You have robbed me of my hen that lays the golden eggs, and now you have taken my harp! When I catch you, I will eat you alive!" The chorus would echo: "When he catches Jack, he will eat him alive!"

During certain dramatic moments a choral response might not be appropriate. If the wolf in "Red Riding Hood" has just said, "The better to gobble you up!" and if he is to spring from her grandmother's bed immediately, the action should not be delayed by having the chorus echo his words. The children can decide if a response would be inappropriate.

Whether or not you dramatize your song plays is optional. This should be an informal activity. Though a character may be singing the same or similar words throughout the song play, he may never improvise the tune the same way twice. If the play is done on several occasions, it will probably always be different.

Creating a Text for a Song Play

You and your class know how to create and write songs. If everyone is interested, why not invent a plot and write words for a dramatic musical? It need not be very long, and it should not be so long that children become discouraged. A song play of a few minutes can be very enjoyable to write and produce.

Whatever the length of your endeavor, the children should be encouraged to create special parts for as many individuals as possible. Stage hands who operate lights and curtains, who make sound effects, etc., are very important. Oftentimes a chorus is essential; songs for this group can narrate much of the action.

When plotting a song play, children should try to think of situations in which something will be repeated. The same song can be used over and over. For instance, there could be people inside several houses, and a character could knock on each door, ask the same question and get the same response. The big bad wolf in "The Three Little Pigs" goes to the home of each little pig and says each time, "I'll huff and I'll puff and I'll blow your house in!" To which each pig replies, "Not by the hair of my chinny chin chin!" Every time the same statement is sung, the same tune would be used.

Or, there could be one central character who encountered several minor characters, as happens in the story of the "Little Red Hen." The hen asks the barnyard animals to help her with the various tasks connected with the growing of wheat which is eventually to become a loaf of bread. Who will help prepare the soil, plant the seed, cultivate the soil, harvest the wheat, thresh it, grind it into flour, make the dough, and bake the bread? To each question the animals respond negatively—until the last question, "Who will help eat the bread?" when they all answer in the affirmative. The same tune can be used for each question; another tune can be used for each response.

Producing the Song Play or Operetta

The staging and presentation of a musical version of a play will be similar to a spoken version, except that you would probably add an instrumental accompaniment to enhance the action and the singing. Rhythm instruments could be used to make some of the sounds of weather—the patter of rain, the boom of thunder, the crack of lightning. Other sounds that can be imitated with instruments include ringing bells or gongs, horses' hoofs on pavement, chugging trains, ticking clocks, and so on.

Most of the songs you and your children will compose will use only two or three different chords for accompaniment. The C chord would begin and end the music, and in between you would need the G_7 (or G) and the F chords. With a little experimenting, perhaps you or some of your older and interested students could find the needed chords on the piano or the Autoharp.

Chapter 2

YOU CAN TEACH RESPONSE TO MUSIC

Whenever a person is within earshot of audible sound, he will react to it, consciously or subconsciously. If it is rhythmical and pleasant, like the kind of music he prefers, he may without thinking tap his toe or nod his head to keep time. He may even regulate his breathing to make it coincide with some of the strong beats. When he marches in a parade or dances to dance music or sings in a community sing, he makes a conscious response.

The power of music to influence behavior is unquestionable. A child, like everyone else, can, and does respond subconsciously to the music he hears. When he goes to the dentist, soothing music may be played to calm him; while he watches a movie or television program, it is the music accompanying the action which heightens the mood. While doing his homework, a school-age child may insist on playing music on a radio. But, if he is subjected to a background of music he does not want to hear—perhaps the sound of a neighbor's radio or someone else's car radio—he may feel discontent, even be irritable.

Why do human beings respond to music sung by the human voice or played on musical instruments? Apparently they find music appealing because it imitates life and living. We can identify four chief areas of imitation. One is the area of *the emotions;* music can imitate people expressing emotions. Another is the area of *natural body rhythms;* there is music which mainly reminds us of these motions. A third is the area of *the senses.* Finally, there is *intellectual stimulation.*

Children can easily detect sounds in music which will remind them of what they hear when people express feelings. Stringed, woodwind or brass instruments, as well as the human voice, can be used to make the listener imagine he is hearing weeping, sighing, calm talk, pleading, laughing, or some other sound of emotion.

Music which is predominantly rhythmical can inspire various movements. An uneven rhythm might imitate the skipping of a person; one slightly different could imitate the gallop of a horse. A strictly even rhythm at walking tempo will suggest walking. But if an urgency is added to the accompaniment of the same music, it will suggest marching with the body erect.

Descriptive music depicts scenes that are usually described in words or pictures, or it imitates the sounds of happenings. Children will easily recognize the rumble of a train, a rooster crowing, the spray of a fountain of water, the ringing of a bell, etc., in descriptive music.

Music that is primarily intellectually stimulating is interesting because of the way it is structured. Perhaps the chief melody weaves around a counter melody; or there is a melody that is disguised behind various clever elaborations; or perhaps one melody is expertly contrasted with another.

It is possible for children to make a conscious response to any of the four types of music. But it is probable that they will find the kind that is chiefly rhythmical and that which describes scenes and events most appealing. They will enjoy miming a fairy tale set to music; they can move like animals to music about those animals; they can become grownups—a policeman directing traffic, a farmwife collecting eggs; they can be falling leaves, chugging trains, Halloween spooks—all to appropriate music.

Whether you are guiding young children to dramatize music or older children to interpret it, you should ask them to be original in their responses. Even if the same response is repeated, it can be done slightly differently each time. If the imitation is of an animal taking a daily walk to a water hole, he might take a different route, sniff at different places, stop to listen for different sounds, etc. The individual will be guided by the music every time, but he will always give his own portrayal.

Try to provide the best possible environment for carrying on response to music. There should be a large clean area, clean enough for the children to perform with shoes off. A rug with little pile is ideal. (A thick pile impedes twirling, galloping and other fast activity.) Furniture should be pushed aside. There should be a record player of the best quality. If your school does not have the records you want, you will find many available free of charge at a public library.

DRAMATIZATION OF MUSIC IN GRADES 1-3

When a music text book is compiled, the authors try to choose music that will appeal to the children for whom it is written. It must be music they can sing with ease and which is also challenging. Some texts are chosen to entertain, perhaps with humor. Others are there to inform the singers about various subjects.

You can use songs to help teach and to increase learning. And when you ask young children to dramatize what they are singing about, it will "come to life" for them. You should ask them to "get inside," to become the thing or character they are portraying. Of course, acting can be done without music. But repetition of motions, and this is what you will be asking your children to do—to behave like elephants or cowboys or snowflakes—such repetition without music can be boring in time. It is the music that makes the difference.

When you choose songs or music for young children to dramatize, be sure there is something going on, some kind of motion. The music should have a distinct, though not necessarily strong, rhythm. It should stimulate movement that is meaningful; motions should not seem silly or unnecessary.

It can be objectionable to have people moving to inspirational or aesthetic music. There might be the added sound of shoes which would spoil the music. Also, a text, for instance, that talks of fields and mountains might be hard to describe with motion. A song like "America, the Beautiful" or Brahms' "Lullaby" should probably be sung just to enjoy the beauty of the words and music.

The categories which have been chosen in the listing below are those most often presented in song books. Items are described and the movement or behavior is discussed in a way that will help you tell your children how the character or object came to move as it does. For example, a train cannot start up quickly because it is heavy; a turtle walks slowly because its legs are suited for swimming and less for walking. If you can arrange it, the children should either actually see whatever they are to portray or see it in moving pictures.

Only songs which are well known or folk songs that can easily be found are given. You will find many other songs in your children's music text books. Sometimes recordings are suggested. If you decide to use any of them, be sure to play only as much of the music as the children need. The whole recording may last too long, and you may notice your group tiring or losing interest after a minute or two. The moment you notice that attention is waning, gradually lower the volume and stop the record.

Moving to Music about Animals, Birds and Insects

Most children have seen, touched, even lived with some of the domesticated animals—both those which are kept as pets and those which are kept to produce food. Or they may have observed animal behavior on television or in motion pictures.

The behavior of any animal, bird or insect depends on the environment in which it finds itself. An animal in a hot climate, for example, will spend a lot of time sleeping. Animals that live in dense jungles will not be able to run as freely as those that live on open plains. Discuss such facts with your children. Ask them to speculate about differences in behavior when the same animal must live in captivity or perform in a circus.

What is important is that your children feel like the creatures they are portraying. They need not try to move on all fours (especially if they might get dirty). Convincing imitations can be done while in an upright position. Children should be discouraged, too, from making too much sound. Usually the music provides enough sound, and only rarely should they add to it. For instance, if the text calls for a cat to meow, this can be pantomimed by raising the head and opening the mouth.

The music should inspire the action. If children become so enthusiastic or excited about what they are doing that they are not staying with the music, stop the activity. Have everyone listen to the music for a few moments without moving. Then have one or more of those who were performing best do it for the others.

If the children are to perform to a song, it may be difficult to both sing and act. In many cases they will have to take turns at being singers and at being performers.

Alligators and Crocodiles. These animals live on both land and in water. Their huge jaws are full of sharp teeth, and when they grab an object and hold it in their jaws, they twist and turn their long bodies. They can break things with their powerful tails. To imitate the jaws the children can join their own hands at the base of the palms for a hinge and move them stiffly up and down.

"The Crocodile Song" (Traditional American).

Ants. These tiny insects live in colonies, never alone. The familiar species tunnel homes in the ground, carrying out grains of dirt one by one, creating a mound around the entrance hole. They march in line when searching for food. Their jaws are strong, and what they carry in them is often larger than themselves.

Bears. These heavy, long-furred animals can stand upright. They are flat-footed, and walking is awkward in the upright position. Bears feed on berries, insects, honey, small game and fish. Yes, they go fishing!

> "The Bear Went Over the Mountain" (Traditional American).
> MacDowell: "Of a Tailor and a Bear." To dramatize this music you will need a tailor, a dancing bear, and a keeper.

Bees. The bee that people see around a flower or blossom is one of thousands of workers from a colony called a hive. Each hive has one queen which lays eggs, one egg in each small wax cell. While a bee is collecting the nectar that will become honey from the center of a flower, it is also collecting pollen, some of which rubs off on and thus pollinates the next flower. When a bee brings the nectar back to the hive, it can inform the other bees of the source by dancing in a circle or a figure eight. They feel the dancing bee with their antennae and learn the direction to go and the distance. A bee stings only to defend its home. Bees make a buzzing sound by moving their wings; they can remain stationary or fly while buzzing.

> Rimsky-Korsakov: "Flight of the Bumblebee."
> Schubert: "The Bee."

Birds. Most birds fly, but they move differently on the ground. A robin, for instance, hops; a pigeon struts; a sandpiper runs. Most larger birds fly by slowly flapping their wings. Many birds use their wings a little, then keep them spread open and soar on currents of air. Some birds flutter their wings almost continually to keep themselves aloft. Most smaller birds eat either seeds and fruit or insects. Larger birds usually catch and eat small game or fish. The bird's bill is used for catching or pecking at food, carrying nest-building materials, carrying food to feed the young, fighting enemies, and so forth.

> "Alouette" (French Canadian Folk Song). This is a cumulative motion song about a meadow lark. The singers say they will pluck its head, beak, neck, back, legs and feet.
> Anderson: "Flying Birds."
> Saint-Saëns: "Aviary" from "Carnival of the Animals"
> Wagner: "Bird Calls" from "Siegfried-Idyll."

Buffaloes, Oxen. The buffalo, or bison, is a wild ox which used to roam the western plains in great herds, grazing on prairie grass. It is a very large animal; a male can weigh more than a ton. When oxen are used as draft animals, they are usually harnessed in pairs to a plow or a wagon with a heavy load. They plod slowly.

> Moussorgsky: "Bydlo, An Old Polish Wagon with Lumbering Wheels Drawn by Oxen" from "Pictures at an Exhibition."

Butterflies, Moths and Caterpillars. The eggs of butterflies and moths become caterpillars. A caterpillar has six front legs and four to ten legs on its abdomen. Caterpillars are variously colored; some have smooth skin, others have a fuzzy covering. They crawl on the ground, on plants and trees, eating leaves and other plant parts until ready to spin an outer casing. The butterfly stays in a chrysalis, the moth in a cocoon until warm weather. Both insects have fragile wings and can use them to float as well as for flying. We see butterflies gathering nectar from flowers during the day. Most moths fly at night.

> Elgar: "Moths and Butterflies" from "Wand of Youth Suite."
> Grieg: "Papillon" ("Butterfly").
> Schumann: "Papillons" ("Butterflies").

Camels. These large animals have one or two humps on their backs. They are used for carrying baggage in desert areas. Usually they walk slowly, but they can also run. Two children can form a four-footed camel. The back child should place his head in the small of the other's back to make the hump and should hold the front child by the waist. By watching the front child's feet, the back child can synchronize the movement of their feet so that both move the same foot at the same time.

Cats and Kittens. These animals are very relaxed and graceful. Their softly padded feet have claws that can be retracted to help them hold onto prey, cling to surfaces, climb trees, etc. They clean their fur by licking it with the tongue or by wetting a front paw and using it to clean hard-to-reach places. Cats stalk prey, crouching and waiting for the best moment to spring up and pounce on it. Kittens prepare for adulthood in play. They like to cuff and chase after scraps of paper, balls, bits of string, etc.

> "The Old Gray Cat" (Folk Song from Alabama).
> "Pussy Cat, Pussy Cat, Where Have You Been?"
> (English Nursery Song).
> "Three Little Kittens" (English Nursery Song).
> Halloween songs about black cats.

Chickens, Hens and Roosters. Domestic fowl spend much of their time pecking at grains and other food, usually on the ground. The hen has a nest or comfortable place in which she lays an egg every day or so. People on the farm then collect the hens' eggs for food. If eggs are not removed from a nest, the hen that laid them will sit on them to keep them warm until baby chicks hatch from them. To get out of its shell each chick must peck the shell until it cracks. The male rooster is a large bird. He crows his "Cockadoodledoo" several times in early morning.

> "I Had a Little Rooster" (American Folk Song).
> "I Love My Rooster" (American Folk Song).
> Moussorgsky: "Ballet of the Unhatched
> Chickens" from "Pictures at an Exhibition."
> Saint-Saëns: "Hens and Cocks" from "Carnival
> of the Animals."

Cows and Bulls. The cow is a large, docile, domesticated animal which spends much of its day standing in a barn or in a field grazing on grass or hay and slowly chewing and re-chewing its food. It has a large bag for a milk gland. Milk is taken by alternately squeezing the four teats. The bull or male cow is more aggressive and may lower its head and charge when angered.

Deer. These timid, gentle animals are usually seen in herds. The males have antlers. They graze on grass and chew their cuds; they also nibble at twigs, nuts, fruits and other wild plants. When frightened, deer will run and bound over bushes and fences with ease. Reindeer, the deer Santa Claus harnesses to pull his sleigh, are used as draft animals by people in the far north of Europe. Other deer include antelopes and caribou; both the male and female of these species have antlers. Elk are large deer; the males have widespreading antlers and thick manes. Largest is the moose; the males' antlers are wide and flat.

> "Jingle Bells" (Pierpont).The tempo of this song is about right for Santa's reindeer.

Dogs, Foxes and Wolves. Everyone who is familiar with dogs will know a lot about foxes and wolves. All of these animals can walk, trot, or run. When cornered or angered, they bare their teeth and growl. Barking or howling are other vocal sounds of these animals. All are hunters. They will watch for prey, standing, sitting or lying motionless with ears pricked. When they are young puppies, they alternate between acting playful and peppy and clamoring for food and taking naps.

> "Oh, Where Has My Little Dog Gone?" (Traditional American).

Ducks, Geese, and Swans. All of these waterfowl have webbed feet. To distinguish them: it is the duck who has a short neck and short legs; the goose has a large, powerful body with strong wings; the swan, also a large bird, has a very long neck and swims gracefully in water. Some ducks and geese are domesticated and are found on farms. The wild varieties can be seen flying; wild geese fly in formation and honk as they fly. Web-footed birds waddle when they walk. A mother duck may be seen leading a line of baby ducks to water to teach them to swim. They obediently follow the lead of the parent during the swimming lesson.

> "Six Little Ducks" (Traditional American).
> "Little Duck," A "Dance-a-Story" record.
> Saint-Saëns: "The Swan" from "Carnival of the Animals."
> Sibelius: "The Swan of Tuonela."
> Tchaikovsky: "Dance of the Swans" from "Swan Lake, Suite from the Ballet." This is the music from Act Two of the ballet.

Elephants. An elephant can weigh six tons—as much as a hundred people! Because it is heavy, it usually walks slowly. It has a long trunk for a nose; the two "fingers" on the end are used both for smelling and picking up food. When looking for food, it will sway back and forth. Every child will know how to put his hands and arms together to make an elephant's trunk.

> Debussy: "Jimbo's Lullaby" from "Children's Corner Suite."
> Saint-Saëns: "The Elephant" from "Carnival of the Animals."

Fish. Fish propel themselves through water by means of fins. They wriggle gracefully when swimming. Children can put their arms to their sides and extend their hands like fins. A fish will investigate the bottom of a pond or other body of water; it will swim alone or with other fish; it will surface with open mouth to get oxygen; and sometimes it makes air bubbles.

> Saint-Saëns: "Aquarium" from "Carnival of the Animals."

Frogs and Toads. Frogs live both on land and in water; they wet themselves from time to time to keep their skin from drying out. Their long hind legs are well developed and enable them to jump long distances. The male frog has a sac in his throat which he inflates with air to make "chug-a-rum" sounds. Toads look similar to frogs, but their bodies are broader. They can live on land.

Giraffes. These long-necked, long-legged animals can get food from the ground or from the treetops. Two children can make one four-legged giraffe. The back child bends over and holds the front child at his waist. The front child must hold his arms close together above his head and with his fingers "nibble" at food.

Goats. The wild mountain goat is sure-footed and can climb up and on steep and craggy places. The domesticated goat eats hay and grass and chews its cud. All goats have horns; sometimes a goat will lower its head to butt an obstruction. The milk of the goat has a stronger taste than that of the cow.

Grasshoppers and Crickets. Both of these insects eat garden crops. Both have wings, and they have long back legs by means of which they can make long jumps. On warm summer nights we hear the field cricket making a shrill chirp. He does this by rubbing his outer wings together.

Hippopotamus and Rhinoceros. Both hippos and rhinos have huge bodies with thick skin, but the hippo has a large head and tiny eyes while the rhino has a proportionately smaller head with one or two horn-like projections on the end of the snout. Both animals are plant eaters; they will charge at other animals, not so much to kill as to defend themselves. Hippos also like to stay in water.

Horses, Donkeys, Ponies and Zebras. These animals are all members of the horse family. They can walk, trot or gallop. They eat hay, grasses, oats and other grains. The horse, donkey and pony are domesticated, and people can ride on them, though sometimes a donkey balks. Donkeys are used as beasts of burden. They have long ears and short manes. The pony is a short-legged horse. The striped zebra is a small wild horse. Among the chief uses of the horse is the roundup of cattle by the cowboy. It can also be harnessed to draw a plow, to pull a wagon, stagecoach, buggy, surrey, and so on. The child who "rides" a "horse" can hold a piece of rope for reins. Both horse and rider should walk, trot or gallop together, keeping time with the music.

> "Camptown Races" (Stephen Foster).
> "Goodbye, Old Paint" and other cowboy songs.
> "She'll Be Comin' 'Round the Mountain" (American Folk Song).
> "Tinga Layo" (Jamaican Folk Song about a donkey).
> Anderson: "Galloping Horses."
> Anderson: "High-Stepping Horses."
> Anderson: "Running Horses."
> Grofé: "On the Trail" from "Grand Canyon Suite."
> Schumann: "The Wild Horseman."

Kangaroos. These are plant-eating animals with short front legs, large, powerful hind legs and a long, strong tail. They can move in long leaps. The mother kangaroo carries her babies in a pouch in front of her abdomen.

> Saint-Saëns: "Kangaroos" from "Carnival of the Animals."

Lions and Tigers. These animals are large cats with traits similar to those of their smaller cousins. Their claws can be retracted;

they are used for climbing, clinging to surfaces, holding prey, etc. They stalk smaller animals for food, springing at and running after them. Their walk is graceful and majestic. Much time is spent stretched out in sleep. The tiger's coat is yellow with black stripes. Lions have a tawny coat and a tuft on the tail. The adult male has a shaggy mane.

>Saint-Saëns: "Royal March of the Lion" from
>"Carnival of the Animals."

Mice and Rats. These small rodents are rarely seen because they move about more at night than in the daytime. They are considered to be pests because they like to live in people's houses. They make holes in walls, build nests, etc. They break into food storage areas and steal food. People use traps to catch rodents; cheese is often used for bait. If a mouse or rat is suddenly seen scampering, many people find this a frightening experience!

>"Hickory, Dickory Dock" (Elliott).
>"The Tailor and the Mouse" (English Folk
>Song).
>"Three Blind Mice" (Old Round).

Monkeys and Chimpanzees. Ask children to act like monkeys, and almost invariably they will proceed to scratch themselves. Primates do spend a lot of time in grooming. In many ways they resemble people, but, because they also walk on all fours, their heads jut forward. Their arms are longer than people's; they are used for climbing trees, swinging from limbs, etc. Monkeys are more active than the larger chimps. When a primate peels a banana or brings food to his mouth with his hand, he seems almost human.

Owls. These large birds are nocturnal and rarely seen. They sit quiet and motionless for long periods of time. With large round eyes, the owl stares straight ahead. To look elsewhere he must turn his whole head; it can be swiveled 180°. The call of most owls is a hoot. The owl preys on small animals and birds which it captures quickly and noiselessly in its strong claws. The food is ripped apart with the hooked beak.

Pigs (Hogs). These fat, heavy, short-legged farm animals are kept for their meat. They can be fattened on garbage, left-over vegetables mixed with water to make swill. Pigs have long snouts and they make loud snorting noises while eating. Piglets squeal; grown pigs grunt in a low pitch, supposedly saying "oink, oink."

Rabbits and Hares. A rabbit is a small hare. Hares have long legs, short tails, and extremely long ears. Their well-developed back legs enable them to make long jumps. A jackrabbit can leap a distance of twenty feet and can run forty miles an hour. True rabbits have shorter legs and move by running or hopping. They dig burrows or make nests under brush piles. In the summer rabbits and hares feed on grass, clover and other plants. In the winter they nibble the bark of tender young trees.

MacDowell: "Of Brer Rabbit."

Seals. These animals have fat, sleek bodies with four webbed feet called flippers, broad fins by which they propel themselves through water. They live chiefly in the cold sea waters of the polar regions where they feed mostly on fish.

Sheep and Lambs. Sheep are timid and docile. They stand in flocks, grazing on grass and chewing their cuds. They are easily led; one will take a notion to move away and the others will follow. The warm, fuzzy fur called wool is shorn and spun into yarn and woven into fabric. Lambs gambol playfully.

"Baa! Baa! Black Sheep" (Elliott).
"Little Bo-Peep" (Elliott).

Snakes and Worms. Because these animals have no legs, they must expand and contract the muscles in their long, slender bodies to get from place to place. They appear to writhe or wriggle. Snakes live under rocks and old logs; they feed on small animals and insects. They have no ears but can detect vibrations in the ground with their whole bodies. Worms burrow into, and aerate, the ground.

Spiders. These are small invertebrate animals, not insects, having eight legs. A silken fiber is secreted from the abdomen to make webs or cocoons. The design of each web varies with the species of spider, but all webs trap food, usually insects which fail to see the fine threads and become caught in the mesh.

"Eency Weency Spider" (North Carolina Folk Song).

Squirrels and Chipmunks. Squirrels are bushy-tailed rodents that live in trees. Their nests can be found in hollow tree trunks or in the forks of trees. Chipmunks, their smaller cousins, have striped cheeks and backs and live in burrows dug in the ground. Both animals eat various fruits, grains, seeds and nuts and hoard food for the winter. Chipmunks are very friendly and can be tamed to take food. They sit on their haunches, holding the food in their front paws. Squirrels chatter; chipmunks say "chuck chuck."

Turkeys. Farmers raise these large, heavy birds for food, especially for Thanksgiving Day. They have a small head and a spreading tail and are said to make a "gobble, gobble" sound. They eat grain, pecking it from the ground.

Turtles. The turtle's body is encased in a hard shell. The humped back is formed from overgrown ribs that are fused together. The under shell is flatter, and the turtle can withdraw his head, four legs and tail inside the two shells. He walks only slowly on land; his short legs are shaped for pushing water when he swims. Turtles have no teeth; they tear but cannot chew food. They eat berries, fruits, insects, worms, etc.

> Saint-Saëns: "Turtles" from "Carnival of the Animals."

Songs and Music about More than One Animal, Bird or Insect

> "Barnyard Song" or "I Bought Me a Cat" (Kentucky Folk Song). A cumulative song about a cat, a hen, a duck, a goose, a sheep, a pig, a cow, a horse, and a dog and the sounds they make.
>
> "The Farmer in the Dell" (American Singing Game). Ask the children chosen to be the characters to act like them.
>
> "The Frog and the Mouse" (American Folk Song). There is a lot of conversation and action in this song about a frog who wooed a mouse and who had to get permission from Uncle Rat to marry her.
>
> "Jig Along Home" (Woody Guthrie). Birds, insects and animals dance with great enthusiasm.
>
> "Little White Duck" (Zaretsky). There are a white duck, a green frog, a black bug, and a red snake in this song.
>
> "Mister Frog Went A-Courtin' " (American Folk Song). Among those attending the wedding of

Mister Frog were a little white moth, a bumble-
bee, a little flea, a pesky old fly, a little red ant,
an old red hen, a nice brown cow, a yellow
chick, an old tom cat, and a big fat snake.

"My Farm" (Argentine Folk Song). On the farm
are a chicken, a dog, a cat, a burro, a duck, and a
pig.

"Old MacDonald" (Traditional American).
MacDonald's farm can have what you want—
chicks, ducks, cows, pigs, geese, etc.

"Over in the Meadow" (Traditional American).
There can be twelve different creatures to
pantomime while singing.

"Noah's Ark" or "One More River to Cross"
(Traditional American). Several different
animals enter Noah's ark.

"The Story of Noah" (John Jacob Niles). The
words are humorous. Several animals are
mentioned.

"The Tailor and the Mouse" (English Folk
Song). The class sings the story while a tailor
and his mouse show the action.

"There Was an Old Woman" (American Folk
Song). The old woman swallowed a fly, a spider,
a bird, a cat, a dog, a goat, a cow—but it was
swallowing a horse that finished her.

"Noah's Ark," A "Dance-a-Story" record.

Prokofief: "Peter and the Wolf." The story is
narrated on all recordings. There is special music
for Peter, a little bird, a cat, a duck, the wolf,
hunters, and grandfather.

Units about Animals, Birds and Insects

By organizing the dramatizations which your children have
been doing into units, you can enhance their study, not only of
musical dramatizations, but also of animals, birds and insects. In a
unit about the farm, for instance, they will have to make a
distinction between sheep and goats, between hens and ducks, etc.

They will appreciate how animals are grouped—to work in a circus, to live in a zoo, to live in natural habitats.

The children might try other methods of dramatization. They might dress in animal, bird or insect costumes. Paper-bag masks make good animal heads. They can make and use hand puppets or stick puppets. The child who feels timid about singing or acting sometimes loses his inhibitions when he can hide himself behind a screen. Puppets that are operated by strings and made to perform on a small stage can also be made to seem realistic. To improve a production, rhythm band and other instruments can be used—wood blocks to imitate the clip clop of horses' hoofs, a drum beating slowly to sound like the heavy thumps of a plodding elephant, etc.

A unit can become a program for entertaining another class, children's parents or even the whole school. The children could improvise a story or it could be written. A narrator could tell the story with the help of a chorus of singers or choral speakers. Let the ideas for units that are sketched below guide you.

Carnival. The animals at a carnival are similar to those at a circus, but they are usually caged for viewing rather than for performing. Amusements at a carnival give the people a chance to participate. There are various kinds of rides—on the merry-go-round, the ferris wheel, and so on. Children ride on ponies. There are games of chance; the person who guesses the number at which the wheel will stop wins a prize. Prizes are also given to those who succeed at games of skill—hitting the moving clown with a ball, shooting a moving duck, proving one's strength, etc. Vendors sell foods like peanuts, hot dogs, candied apples, spun sugar. You will find songs in your music texts about such activities.

Circus. At a circus people and animals perform for an audience. The show could start with a march by all performers. Then each performer could do his special act. Larger animals like bears, elephants, lions and tigers might be made to climb on boxes and balance in some way. Small dogs and horses might be expected to rear up and walk on their hind legs. Some animals might jump through hoops. Horses would jump over high hurdles. Seals would balance balls on their noses. Chimpanzees could roller skate. Clowns would behave in ridiculous ways—falling and tumbling. Jugglers could toss balls and rings. Trapeze artists would swing from bars in the air. (Children could hold bars over their heads, run forward and back, etc.)

"The Man on the Flying Trapeze" (American Circus Song).

Kabalevsky: "Comedians' Galop."

MacDowell: "Clown."

Pinto: "Run, Run." (Trapeze artists run and sway.)

Rimsky-Korsakov: "Dance of the Tumblers" from "Snow Maiden."

Smetana: "Dance of the Comedians" from "The Bartered Bride."

Shostakovitch: "Polka" from "The Age of Gold" ballet. (This is music for clowning.)

Stravinsky: "Circus Polka."

Country Fair. Farmers bring their best animals and fowl to a fair where they are judged and awarded prizes for excellence. There might be pens of chickens, hens, roosters, ducks, geese, turkeys, cows, bulls, goats, oxen, horses, pigs, rabbits, sheep and lambs. The animals could be walked around in a field and inspected by judges who would award prizes. The judges could also decide the winners of other events—best grown fruits, vegetables, best pies, cakes, bread and other baked goods, best-made clothing, and so on. Tractors and farm machinery could be on display. A fair can be what you want it to be. There should be entertainment, such as races. At the end, everyone could join in a square dance.

"Come to the Fair" (Music by Easthope Martin).

Farm. Most modern farmers specialize in the raising of live-stock or garden produce. Only in the barnyard of an old-fashioned farm do we see a variety of domestic animals and fowl. A farmer might have chickens, hens, roosters, ducks, geese, turkeys, bees, cows, bulls, goats, horses, pigs, rabbits, sheep and lambs. There would be dogs, cats and kittens. Mice and rats might live in the barn with spiders and other wild creatures. Activities would include caring for the domestic animals—keeping them under shelter, feeding and watering them—and taking the produce—milking cows and goats, shearing sheep, collecting eggs, etc.

Nature Trail or Park. On a walk through a park or other nature walk one will see various kinds of birds. There will be bees, butterflies and moths in the warmer weather. In the grass and on walkways there should be ants, grasshoppers, crickets, caterpillars,

snakes, worms, spiders, and turtles. Squirrels and chipmunks might
be scampering amongst the trees. On ponds, pools and brooks will be
seen wild ducks and geese, fish and frogs.

It can be fun to bring a picnic to a park. Everyone can feed
birds, squirrels and chipmunks. The children can play in the playground areas. The youngest will use the equipment—swings, seesaws,
slides, sand piles, jungle gyms, and so on. They might play with their
toys—wagons, small trucks, doll carriages, etc. Others might use roller
skates, bicycles, ice skates, sleds, toboggans, whatever suits the
season. Tennis and badminton and volleyball would be played on
courts, baseball and softball on diamonds. There would be swimming
in the pool. Horseback riders might come by on a trail. Other
children's activities include social games—follow the leader, hide-and-
seek, hop scotch, marbles, jump-rope, ball bouncing, etc.

> "Feed the Birds" from "Mary Poppins."
> "The Happy Wanderer" (Music by F. Möller)
> (for hiking).
> "See Saw, Margery Daw" (Elliott).
> Moussorgsky: "Tuileries" ("Children at Play")
> from "Pictures at an Exhibition."
> Schubert: "March Militaire" (for follow-the-
> leader).
> Schubert: "Waltzes, Nos. 1 and 2, Opus 9A"
> (for swinging. Two children stand, join hands to
> make the swing seat. Another child pushes the
> "seat," runs under it, turns, pushes it again and
> runs under, turns and repeats.)
> Strauss, J., Jr.: "On the Beautiful Blue Danube"
> Waltzes (for ball bouncing, for skating, etc.):

Zoo. In the best modern zoos animals are no longer confined
to cages. They are now housed in areas closely resembling the areas
of the world from which they came. Children who dramatize the
behavior of zoo animals can pretend they are in their natural
habitats. Swans, owls and various birds would be found in the aviary.
There would be an aquarium of fish. Among the animals would be
alligators, crocodiles, bears, buffalo, deer, donkeys, foxes, wolves,
elephants, giraffes, hippopotamuses, rhinoceros, lions, tigers,
monkeys, chimpanzees, seals, snakes, and turtles.

Moving to Music as Phenomena in Nature

Music text books have many songs about natural events, and there are many musical compositions which describe the activity of the wind, the ocean, storms, the movement of trees—phenomena that can be heard or that have movement. A few of the happenings in nature are listed below, and songs and music are suggested. In many cases the recording is too long. It should be played for about a minute, the volume slowly turned down and the playing stopped.

Trees and Falling Leaves. Discuss the different shapes of trees with the children. Some are tall and slender; some are heavily branched; some shaped like a cone, and so on. Two or three children can stand back to back so that their bodies make the trunk and their extended arms the branches. Single children can make small trees. They can hold their arms up for a short period of time.

When a leaf falls, it never comes straight down. It will twist and turn, blown up, then down, by gusts of wind. Children can be leaves, lightly touching the branches of a "tree" until "wind" blows them off. Children who are the wind can chase and blow them again, finally allowing them to settle on the ground.

"The Tree in the Wood" (English Folk Song).

To give the effect of leaves being blown about, someone can strum back and forth on the strings of an autoharp without pressing chord bars.

Respighi: "The Pines of the Villa Borghese"
from "The Pines of Rome."
Strauss, J., Jr.: "Tales of the Vienna Woods."
Wagner: "Forest Murmurs" from "Siegfried"
opera.
Williams, R.: "Autumn Leaves."

Wind, Rain and Storms. Sometimes wind is a gentle breeze. It can whistle through trees. Sometimes it comes in sudden, heavy gusts, dislodging objects and rattling things that are ordinarily stationary. Wind can sound like a long roar.

Some children can be trees, buildings and other immobile objects. Others can be windmills. Several children can be wind. When the music indicates that the wind is strong, they can blow at the various objects. Because wind always comes from one direction, the group representing wind may need a leader. He should be a child who listens well to the music.

When rain pours, it pelts on surfaces with a steady tapping sound. The sound of feet tapping like rain can be amplified by the tapping of several rhythm sticks. Some music about rain may remind children of splashing in puddles and watching water spray.

When music depicts a storm, the rain usually starts gradually. There is one rain drop, then another and another. One child can spring up and "plop." The music will tell everyone how fast to go, when to come in, how often, etc. If it is a wild storm, the wind may blow the rain drops and make them fall at a slant.

> "The Wind Blew East" (Folk Song from the Bahamas)
> Britten: "Storm," the fourth "Sea Interlude" from "Peter Grimes" opera.
> Debussy: "Gardens in the Rain."
> Grofé: "The Storm" from "Grand Canyon Suite."
> Rossini: "The Storm" from "William Tell Overture."

Ocean Waves. The rolling of ocean waves is incessant; the force with which they hit beaches, rocks, etc., varies. When the weather is calm, they swish gently; when it is stormy, they roar and crash.

When they respond to music about ocean waves, children might hold hands in a line. (It need not be straight.) With arms raised, they would run forward like a long wave rolling toward the beach. When the music indicates the breaking of the wave, they should curl arms and torsos down like a wave curling over. To show how the water recedes, they could stay down and run backwards.

> Bloch: "Waves" from "Poems of the Sea."
> Debussy: "La Mer."
> "At the Beach," a "Dance-a-Story" record.

Snow and Winter. Snowflakes are very light and are easily tossed by faint gusts of wind. They whirl about as if dancing on their way to the ground. Children play with fallen snow, forming it into sculpture like a snow man or a snow maiden. They make snow balls and snow forts and have snowball fights. They slide, toboggan and ski on snow. Everyone shovels snow off sidewalks and driveways. In the days before the automobile, people rode in sleighs pulled by horses, often with bells jingling merrily.

In winter the ponds and other large bodies of water freeze and people skate on the ice. Jack Frost is supposed to come quietly on cold winter nights and sketch pictures on window panes with his paint brush full of frost.

"Frosty, the Snowman" (Nelson and Rollins).

"Jingle, Bells!" (J. Pierpont).

Debussy: "The Snow Is Dancing" from "Children's Corner Suite."

Mozart: "Sleigh Ride" from "German Dances" (K. 605, No. 3).

Tchaikovsky: "Troika en Traineaux" ("In a Three-Horse Sleigh.")

Waldteufel: "Skaters' Waltz."

Moving to Music about People at Work

There are numerous songs in music text books about community helpers—firemen, policemen, etc. The work of people such as carpenters when they handsaw or hammer is also described in song, since the motions they make are done in rhythm. Only those occupations which are commonly sung about have been chosen for description.

Barber or Hairdresser. The customer is shown to a chair, and his shoulders are covered. The barber snips, snips and brushes the cuttings off the person's shoulders. The hairdresser puts strands of hair on curlers and has the customer sit under a dryer. Eventually he combs out the hair. The customer pays and leaves.

Carpenter. The carpenter measures and marks a board. He lays it on sawhorses and saws back and forth. Then he holds it at the place it will go and hammers nails into it. After several boards are in place, the carpenter might sand them with a piece of sandpaper.

"Bling Blang" (Woody Guthrie).

Farmer or Farm Woman. Activities are different on the different kinds of farms. There are garden farms, egg-producing farms, beef farms, horse farms, milk-producing farms, hog farms, and so on. On an old-fashioned all-purpose farm with many different kinds of animals (described on page 65) chores would be diversified. Not only would the animals have to be tended, cows milked, eggs collected, sheep shorn, and so forth; the farmer might have to grow hay and grains. He would drive a tractor and use it for plowing a garden, harrowing, planting, cultivating, and perhaps for harvesting. Picking fruits and vegetables by hand would be a rhythmic activity which could be done to music.

> Debussy: "The Little Shepherd" from
> "Children's Corner Suite."
> Grieg: "Cow Keeper's Tune" from "Norwegian
> Melodies, Op. 63."
> Schumann: "The Happy Farmer" from "Album
> for the Young."

Fireman. When a fireman is on duty, he stays in the fire-house. When the signal sounds, he rushes to the fire truck, either to drive it or to ride to the fire. On the scene, he attaches a hose to a hydrant; he holds the other end and aims it at the burning building. He might use an axe to break a window or door so as to get inside and rescue people who are unable to get out.

Mother. An old-fashioned mother scrubs clothes by hand, hangs them on a clothesline, then irons them. She cooks and bakes and serves meals. She washes and dries dishes, sweeps the floors, vacuums rugs, dusts and polishes furniture. She sews clothing.

> "Here We Go 'Round the Mulberry Bush"
> (American Folk Song).

Nurse or Doctor. Sometimes a nurse or doctor helps a sick person, someone who has broken a bone or has something else wrong. At other times he or she checks to see if you are well. He makes you open your mouth and looks inside. He looks in your eyes and in your ears. He holds your wrist to take your pulse. He puts his stethoscope on different places on your chest and back.

Policeman or Police Woman. Most songs about police are about those who direct traffic. School traffic guards are not police, but they help children cross the street. The person holds up a hand to stop cars; then with his other hand he signals pedestrians to cross. When everyone is safely across, he signals the cars to go. If he directs traffic at a crossroad, he must stop one set of traffic, allowing the other to go. In time, he alternates the procedure.

Postman. The man who delivers mail on foot carries it in a large heavy bag slung over his shoulder and hanging at his side. As he continues to deliver pieces of mail, the bag becomes lighter, and he can straighten up. A postman walks in regular rhythm.

Many songs for Valentine's Day are about the postman.

Salesperson. In a department store the salesperson shows the customers his wares. They choose what to buy and pay for it. At the gas station the attendant asks the customer what he wants. He holds the pump hose at the gas tank, and he returns it to the pump. He lifts the car hood to check the oil and water; he wipes the car windshield. The customer pays him. In the grocery store the stock boys bring boxes, bags, cans, jars, vegetables and fruits from the stock rooms and fill the shelves. Customers push carts down the aisles, load them with items, and pay the cashier.

Serviceman or Woman. When we see the person who is in service, he or she is usually in a uniform, perhaps marching in a parade held in honor of a national holiday. Children can march like soldiers, sailors, marines, Waves, Wacs, etc. Some could carry flags. Some could pretend to play bugles and others could tap on drums.

> "When Johnny Comes Marching Home" (Lambert).
>
> Sousa: "Semper Fideles" (or any appropriate march music).

Other Occupations. Other work that can be done in response to music includes baking—stirring the dough, rolling it out, putting it in the pan, putting the pan in the oven; painting a house or room; mending shoes—taking off the worn sole or heel and nailing on the new ones; working with a pick and shovel; and playing professional tennis or other sport.

> "I've Been Workin' on the Railroad" (Traditional).
>
> "Whistle While You Work" from "Snow White and the Seven Dwarfs."
>
> Mozart: "Eine Kleine Nachtmusik." The first movement would be suitable for moderately fast work; the second can be used for slow work; the fourth movement would suit very fast work.
>
> Mozart: "German Dance, No. 7" (K. 605, No. 2).

Moving to Music about Vehicles of Transportation

There are a number of songs for young children about trains, boats, bicycles and other vehicles. The songs describe them and talk about how they work, how they are operated, etc.

Airplanes. Children can easily stretch their arms straight out to the sides and run forward in time with music about airplanes. When they turn, they wheel about, as if turning on an axis. They must bank to turn left or turn right. Both a takeoff and a landing are done slowly. Airplanes carry passengers and cargo.

Automobiles, Trucks and Buses. The children can sit in their seats and pretend to be driving. Their feet will operate pedals. Their hands will be used for shifting, steering, tooting the horn, etc. The bus driver stops at bus stops, takes fares, makes change, asks passengers to move back, and so on.

Bicycles. The children can sit at their seats and pretend to hold handlebars. They would rock back and forth in rhythm with the music, pretending to press pedals. They should signal to make turns.

Boats and Ships. Canoes and small boats can be rowed with paddles or oars. Children may row at their desks. To paddle a canoe, the person pushes first on one side of the boat, then the other, using only one paddle. The oarsman of a rowboat uses two oars, one in each hand. He bends forward and pulls back against the water.

While singing a sea chantey or a song about a large ship, the children could pantomime doing some of the chores of sailors. They could scrub decks, polish brass, pump out water that has sprayed inboard, hoist sails, lower sails, drop anchor, wind up anchor, load and unload cargo by standing in line and passing the goods from person to person. While on board ship, people may have to work to keep their balance as the ship rocks back and forth. Sailors who have been at sea may swagger at first when they start to walk on land.

> "Blow, Ye Winds" and other sea chanteys.
> "Row, Row, Row Your Boat" (Round).
> Kullak: "Boating on the Lake."
> Offenbach: "Barcarolle" from "Tales of Hoffmann."

Trains. When you choose children to make a "train," choose a good leader to be the engine. He can be followed by any number of cars—a coal car, freight or baggage cars, passenger cars, a caboose at the end. "Cars" would hold onto each other at the waist (or by the shoulders). If it is a passenger train, a conductor could call: "All aboard! All aboard!" when it is time to go. A bell could be rung. The music would start slowly. Feet shuffling on a bare floor sound like the swishing and hissing of a train. When going full speed (this should never be so fast that the children lose control), have someone tap rhythm sticks to imitate the clicking of the wheels on the tracks. Someone can make a few high-pitched "Toot! Toot!" 's before "crossroads." As the music nears the end, the destination should be in sight; the train should gradually slow and come to a full stop.

> "Down by the Station" (Round).
> "Git on Board" (American Spiritual).
> "Train Is a-Comin' " (American Spiritual).
> "When the Train Comes Along" (American Spiritual).
> Honegger: "Pacific 231."
> Villa-Lobos: "Little Train of the Caipira."

Moving to Music about Holidays

Holidays like Christmas and Thanksgiving are times for singing. There are many songs about Halloween, Valentine's Day and many of the other holidays which can be dramatized.

Halloween. Black cats prowl. They crouch; they arch their backs, ready to spit and fight. Pumpkin people wear faces with funny or scary expressions. In the darkness, owls hoot and bats fly. Ghosts, goblins, ghouls and other spooks float through the sky. Witches in black ride broomsticks. Skeletons appear; knockings are heard.

> Grieg: "March of the Dwarfs."
> MacDowell: "Villain" from "Marionettes."
> MacDowell: "Witch" from "Marionettes."
> Moussorgsky: "A Night on Bald Mountain."
> Saint-Saëns: "Dance Macabre."
> Saint-Saëns: "Fossils" from "Carnival of the Animals."

Thanksgiving. Before Thanksgiving Day, turkeys strut in the barnyard. On the first Thanksgiving, Indians who had helped the Pilgrims survive dined with them. Everyone was grateful for what they had. Then and now people walk to church.

Among the activities of the Indians would be walking through the forest, hunting with bow and arrow, planting and harvesting crops, grinding corn, dancing, weaving blankets, singing, playing drums and other instruments.

"Over the River" (Traditional Song).
Cadman: "Thunderbird Suite" (based on American Indian tunes).
Griffes: "Two Sketches Based on Indian Themes."
MacDowell: "From an Indian Lodge" from "Woodland Sketches."

Hanukah. This Hebrew holiday is also called the Festival of Lights. Over twenty centuries ago, after the Jews had driven their enemy out of Israel, only one day's supply of oil was left to light the Menorah, the holy candelabrum. Miraculously, the oil lasted eight days. Eight candles are lighted, one for each day of Hanukah. Children play with the dreydl, a four-sided top. Gifts are exchanged.

Christmas. Many aspects of this holiday can be dramatized, ranging from the story of the birth of Christ to the more amusing tales of the doings of Santa Claus. A few possibilities are discussed below.

"The Friendly Beasts" (Old English Carol). On the night Jesus was born, the various animals in the stable each played a part in the event. Children can act out the stanzas about each animal. A chorus would sing the first stanza, the donkey the second, the cow the third, the sheep the fourth, the dove the fifth, and the chorus would sing the last.

" 'Twas the Night Before Christmas" (Music by Darby). You could play the recording and have the action pantomimed.

"O, Christmas Tree" (German Carol). You could begin your dramatization with a child as a fir tree standing in the woods. A family could arrive and chop it down, carry it home. There everyone would help decorate it. When it was ready, the people could join hands and dance around it. Then they could sing songs of the season.

Tchaikovsky: "The Nutcracker Suite." (See the book, "The Nutcracker," by Warren Chappell.) To dramatize the whole story you would need a narrator, at least three main characters—Marie, the

Nutcracker Prince, the wicked Mouse King, and various groups of toy soldiers, mice and dancers. During the playing of "Overture Miniature," the narrator would tell of the Christmas Eve party at Marie's home. Later Marie would carry her favorite gift, a nutcracker in the shape of a man, to the toy cupboard. Thereafter the story would concern Marie's dream—the fight of Nutcracker and the Mouse King. During the playing of "Marche," toy soldiers would fight with the mice. Once the Mouse King was defeated, Nutcracker would turn into a handsome Prince and invite Marie to the Kingdom of Sweets. There the Sugar Plum Fairy and her attendants would dance, and Marie and the Nutcracker Prince would watch dolls from Russia ("Trepak"), Arabia ("Arabian Dance"), China ("Chinese Dance"), and the toy flutes ("Dance of the Flutes") dance. At the end, flowers would dance "Waltz of the Flowers."

Valentine's Day. Have the children sing a song that has a walking rhythm. They can take turns being the postman delivering Valentines.

Moving to Motion Songs

Most of the motions pertain to the words of the songs, but some are done just for fun. This kind of response to music is guaranteed to remove the apathy from a group of indifferent children.

> "Chiapanecas" (Mexican Clapping Song). Singers clap twice during the rests.
>
> "Clap Your Hands" (American Folk Song). Singers can clap the rhythm of this old square dance tune.
>
> "If You're Happy" (Traditional). On the first stanza singers clap hands, second they nod heads, third tap toes, and on the fourth they do all three motions together.
>
> "Kuckuck" ("The Cuckoo") (Austrian Folk Song). On the chorus singers slap knees, clap hands and snap fingers.
>
> "The Noble Duke of York" (Play Party Song). When the word "up" is sung, everyone stands; on the word "down," they sit.

"This Old Man" (English Folk Song). On the ten short stanzas singers touch their thumbs, shoes, knees, and so on.

"Under the Spreading Chestnut Tree" (Old English Folk Song). Motions require singers to bend down, spread arms like branches, tap chest and head (nut), and hold arms overhead.

Moving to Music about Playing Musical Instruments

This activity will help children appreciate the work of instrumentalists and interest them in future study. Before you ask them to "play" any instrument, the children should either have seen that instrument actually played or watched it being played in a movie. Since most instruments are played sitting down, this activity can be done in seats or at desks. You will find numerous opportunities to have children "play" along with records not listed here. Usually one minute, maybe two, is long enough.

"Instrument Song" (Austrian Folk Song).

"Johnny Schmoker" (Pennsylvania Dutch Folk Song).

"Oh, Susanna" (S. Foster). While children are singing, they can pretend to be strumming a guitar or a banjo.

"Two Musicians" ("The German Band") (German Folk Song).

Debussy: "Doctor Gradus ad Parnassum" from "Children's Corner Suite." (A pianist seems to be practicing scales.)

Saint-Saëns: "Pianists" from "Carnival of the Animals."

Moving to Music about Children's Toys and Games

You will find that many of the songs in music text books for children are about their play, about toys like the rocking horse, a doll, a ball or building blocks, or about games like hide-and-go-seek or tag. Famous composers who were fond of children have written descriptive music about their toys and games.

"Ride a Cock Horse" (J.W. Elliott).

Bizet: "Jeux d'Enfants" ("Children's Games").

This suite has the titles "Trumpet and Drum" (children play at being soldiers), "Doll's Lullaby," "The Top," "Little Husband and Wife," and "Galop" (dance).

Debussy: "Serenade for the Doll" from "Children's Corner Suite." The serenade might be sung by a boy doll under the window of a girl doll. He might be strumming a guitar.

Debussy: "Golliwogg's Cake Walk" from "Children's Corner Suite." A golliwogg was a funny-faced doll with mop hair who wore a bright coat and striped pants. A cakewalk was a dance made up by people dancing around a table with a big cake in the middle. The dancer who made up the funniest dance won the cake.

Gounod: "Funeral March of a Marionette."

Herbert: "March of the Toys" from "Babes in Toyland."

Liadoff: "The Music Box."

Pierné: "March of the Little Lead Soldiers."

Poldini: "Dancing Doll."

Rossini: "La Boutique Fantasque" ("The Magic Toy Shop"). In the arrangement of the ballet music by Respighi there are six movements. The "Overture" sounds mysterious, as if the toys were coming to life. Italian dolls whirl in a "Tarantella," after which Polish dolls dance the slow, stately "Mazurka." Russian boy dolls with arms folded stamp and do knee bends to "Cossack Dance." Then girl dolls hop on one leg and kick the other high to the music of "Can-Can." Toy horses respond to the last piece, "Galop."

Schumann: "Knight of the Hobby Horse" from "Album for the Young."

Schumann: "Soldier's March" from "Album for the Young."

Tchaikovsky: "Dolly's Funeral" from "Children's Album."

Tchaikovsky: "Soldier's March" from "Children's Album."

INTERPRETATION OF MUSIC IN GRADES 4-6

If older children have had experience in dramatizing songs and music through the years, it will be easy for them to use their bodies to interpret various kinds of music. They will continue to create dramatizations for descriptive music, music that reminds the listener of the behavior of animals, people at work, and so on. They can also respond to music that is chiefly or entirely rhythmic. What may be new with older children is an ability to interpret music that imitates people expressing emotions, and music that is written to appeal to the intellect.

Songbooks for children in the intermediate grades will have fewer songs for interpretation. You will need to use recordings, a few of which are suggested below. Also, the children can respond to rhythms played on instruments, particularly drums.

Activities should be conducted in a large enough space to allow everyone to move freely. If necessary, make rules before starting. Each child may move in the direction of his choice (unless you direct otherwise) as long as he does not bump into or touch anyone else. If someone notices that he is about to collide with someone else, he should mark time in place until there is space to move.

If you notice during an interpretive activity that the children are tiring or seem bored, gradually soften the volume of the music and bring it to a stop. If you anticipate before starting the activity that the children may tire of the sameness or may become physically exhausted, divide the class into two or more groups and have them respond alternately.

Responding to Rhythm Instruments

If it is available, use a two-headed bongo drum. Or have on hand two or more drums with different pitches. Other combinations of instruments might be rhythm sticks and wood blocks, a large glass and a small glass, a cymbal and a triangle. High and low pitches can be played on a piano or a xylophone.

The Magic Drum. If children are responding to instruments for the first time, start with an exercise like this one, using one drum or other instrument. Have the poem on the chalk board.

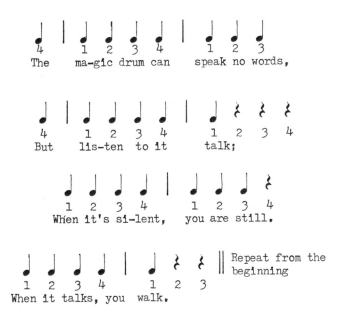

Have everyone read the poem together. Have it read a second time, asking that everyone read it in rhythm. The third time it is spoken, have everyone clap on each word or syllable. Hands should be held open, palms up on the rests. On the fourth reading, have the children stand at their places and step the words and syllables. On rests they should stand without moving.

As soon as the children have the idea, invite someone to play the rhythm of the words on a drum (or a cluster of low notes on a piano if no drum is available). The person thinks the words without saying them. The other children should walk the rhythm, stepping on words and syllables and stopping on rests.

As another part of the exercise, tell the children to change the direction in which they are walking at the end of each phrase. This means that they will walk straight ahead in one direction on the first phrase, turn on the word "But" to walk in a second direction for the second phrase, and so forth.

High Drum, Low Drum. In this exercise instruments with two different pitches will "command" the listeners to move first in one way, then in another. You could start with children seated. Give directions. For example, tell them that you will play a "message" on two different drums. Whatever you play on the low-pitched drum they must "play" by slapping their thighs, and what you play on the high-pitched drum they should clap. They start the moment you finish. If they have done it correctly, you will give another "message." (In the examples below, notes with "low" heads, stems going up, can be played on one drum; notes with heads "high" on the other.)

Next, try a few messages with high and low in the same measure.

Now change the directions. For example, have everyone walk the messages. They could stamp the low sounds, tiptoe the high. Or they might walk the low sounds, stop and clap the high.

Let the children take turns inventing two-measure messages on the drum. If everyone is doing well, add a third activity. To get a third sound, use a drum stick and tap on the rim of the drum.

Moving to Music

Before you play the recording of the music the children will be interpreting, give the title and, if it is descriptive music, tell them the story or picture the composer had in mind. Then play the record. Ask the children what the music described and discuss what they thought was happening. If possible, the music should be heard two or three times before the children try to move to it.

There may be times when you may want to assign your class to do a pantomime to music. For example, to help everyone appreciate the struggle of a moth from a cocoon, you might first show a movie of such an event. Then you could play a very slow, quiet composition like Debussy's "Prelude to the Afternoon of a Faun" or Bach's "Air for the G String" and let the music help the children do a slow pantomime.

Some of the music which you will ask your children to interpret may have been written for intellectual listening. A title like "Andante," for instance, would not give anyone a clue about what is to be pictured or what kind of action the music is depicting. Each interpreter will need to listen carefully to the music to determine the mood, whether or not it is expansive, requiring a lot or a little space, if it is flowing music or detached, and so on. The children should hear such music as many times as necessary before they attempt to move to it.

Moving to music is not just moving feet in time. Remind the children as needed that it includes moving the arms, the torso, the head, the hands, the whole body. Free interpretation allows for much variation. There is no one "right" way. The same person, moving to the same composition several times, may do it differently each time. No two people need interpret it the same.

Bizet: "L'Arlesienne Suites, Nos. 1 and 2." Each suite has four parts, each based on old French songs and dances. Each part can be presented in a separate lesson, though in the interest of saving time you may want to play large segments of each suite to give the children a chance to become familiar with it. All of the pieces are rhythmic, and it will be easy to feel a response to the various tempos. In some parts the children will hear two melodies playing at the same time. For example, in "Carillon," the fourth part of Suite No. 1, the bells are heard in walk rhythm. At a higher pitch is the music of a gay dance. (If they listen carefully they will hear the third theme.) The class should be divided into as many groups as there are melodies, and each group should interpret its melody.

Copland: "Billy the Kid" ballet. This is a story about the old west, told in music. There is a lot of American folk music, especially cowboy tunes, used. The story takes place in a frontier town. When twelve-year-old Billy sees his mother killed during a street fight, he stabs the killer. There is a card game and scenes of Billy's imprisonment and escape, the hunt by the posse, and their discovery of the outlaw.

Dukas: "The Sorcerer's Apprentice." In his master's absence the young apprentice to a magician uses words of magic and brings a broom to life. He commands it to bring him some water. When he has enough, the apprentice tries to stop it, but, unfortunately he does not know the magic words. While the broom works on, he chops it in half with an axe. Instead of stopping, the two halves of the broom continue to bring water. The room is flooded. Finally the sorcerer returns and speaks the magic words to stop the broom.

Grieg: "Peer Gynt Suite No. 1." The composer wrote several pieces as incidental music for an Ibsen play, and in this suite are four of the pieces. Peer Gynt is a scoundrel, a liar, and a conceited, disrespectful fellow. He is sought as an outlaw for all his wrongdoings. In "Morning Mood" the composer has described the beauty and tranquility of the Norwegian countryside. "Ase's Death" is sweetly sad. Peer has returned from his travels to find his mother dying. To cheer her he tells her that he will take her by sleigh to a banquet in a great castle. "Anitra's Dance" is a dance by the beautiful daughter of an Arab chief who cunningly steals Peer's money and his horse. "In the Hall of the Mountain King" is music that describes the kingdom of the Trolls. Peer is almost changed into a gnome when he tries to control them.

Humperdinck: Selections from "Hansel and Gretel" opera. Be sure the children know the version of the story used by the composer. In this account the parents love their children. While they are in the woods picking strawberries, they become lost. The Sandman shakes sand on their eyes and fourteen angels watch over them as they sleep. A Dew Fairy awakens them and they discover a gingerbread house which they start to nibble. The owner, a witch, has control of them until Gretel pushes her into her own oven. This frees all the gingerbread children. Hansel and Gretel's parents find them, and there is a joyous reunion.

Kodaly: Suite from "Háry János" opera. Háry János is an old soldier from Hungary. Every day he spins yarns about himself, wild stories of his deeds as a handsome youth. Amongst the stories is one about the wife of Napoleon and how she falls in love with him. Napoleon is so angry he sends his army to deal with him. But János singlehandedly defeats them all, then overcomes Napoleon. He enters Vienna in triumph and takes over the emperor's throne.

Prokofief: Suite from "Love for Three Oranges," an opera. The opera tells the story of the prince who is so sad he cannot laugh. He can be cured only by finding three oranges. These are magic fruit inside of which are three princesses. When the prince finds the orange grove, he cuts the oranges with his sword. He loves and marries the most beautiful princess. The villains who committed the evil are discovered and sentenced to hang. But they escape by jumping through a trap door on the stage.

Sibelius: "The Swan of Tuonela." According to Finnish legend the land of death is called Tuonela. Around this land are the black waters of a fast-moving river on which the swan floats majestically.

Smetana: "The Moldau." The music describes the most important river in Bohemia, a province of Czechoslovakia. The composer takes the listeners on a trip starting at the source of the river, describing incoming streams, the sounds of a hunting party, dancing at a village wedding, the river by moonlight, the water going over rapids, and finally the river passing an old fortress.

Strauss, Richard: "Till Eulenspiegel's Merry Pranks." Till is a practical joker of German folklore who, by picking on authoritarian figures, is something of a hero. In the music we hear him ride his horse through the market place upsetting and breaking the pots and pans. Next, he puts on the robes of a priest and pretends to be virtuous. He falls in love, but the girl rejects him. He meets a group of pedagogues and pretends to be a professor. It sounds as if he skips away and whistles a happy tune. Finally, the authorities chase and catch Till and there is serious music, as if he is being tried for his pranks. He laughs, but in the end he supposedly is hanged. The music seems to say: "Or was he? . . . "

Tchaikovsky: Suite from "The Sleeping Beauty" ballet. At the christening of Princess Aurora six good fairies each step forward to offer her a gift. One fairy who was not invited comes and puts a curse on the baby. This is fulfilled when Aurora is sixteen. She pricks her finger and falls asleep. Then the Lilac Fairy waves her wand and everyone in the palace is made to sleep. A hundred years later, Prince Charming finds the palace of sleeping people. He wakes the sleeping princess with a kiss, and everyone joins in dancing and festivities.

CREATING DANCE IN GRADES 1-6

When people dance, they formalize the movements they naturally make when they feel happy. The elated person may skip, jump up and down, clap hands, twirl, and so forth. Folk dances are made up of motions like these. If your children have participated in dancing, they will be familiar with the steps and motions.

Dance music is not always for dancing; some was written for people to hear while they were sitting. Dance-type music reminds us of the happiness and other good feelings it was written to commemorate. Names like waltz, mazurka, gigue, minuet, etc., appear in both old and modern suites, groups of pieces. Other music has been written in dance rhythm and given other names—perhaps a movement of a symphony or part of a tone poem. Many of the children's songs which are usually only sung can also be danced because they, too, are in dance rhythm.

The music you will ask the children to dance to will be folk songs and simple music with an even beat. There should not be a large variety of themes or rhythms, as there would be, for example, in a movement of a symphony or a sonata. Because the music is simple, the dancers will decide on one or two steps and motions and repeat these during at least a long segment of the music, if not for the whole piece.

How will your children know what foot patterns, body motions, and head and hand positions to choose? You can begin by asking them to think of basic steps. They should mention walking (or stepping), skipping, galloping, running, "skating," hopping, and jumping. These are ways of moving the feet that are used in dances like the waltz, polka, minuet, square dance, fox trot, and various folk dances, singing games, and contemporary dances. For example, the person who can gallop can do the polka.

Ask the children to discuss some of the motions that are parts of dances. They should mention putting hands on hips and twisting, swinging the arms up and down, clapping the hands, turning the head and glancing down, and combinations such as having one hand on a hip, the other out to the side, etc. Ask them what motions can be done by two people that would be different from the motions of a single person. What patterns could a group of people make?

When you choose music for your children to dance to, try to find songs or compositions that are in three parts. For example, "Twinkle, Twinkle, Little Star" has one kind of music for the first two lines; there is a different sound for the next two lines; and the last two lines sound like the first two. It is customary to name the parts with letters of the alphabet. We would say that the song is in three-part form, with a pattern of A B A. When the children make up dances to three-part form, they should hear the return of the first part and use the same motions at the end as they did in the beginning. If the music is in two parts, they should change motions when the second part comes in.

A possible procedure for creating a dance would be to have the children sing the song or listen to the music you are to use and have them move their arms, hands, torsos and heads. You might talk about possible foot movements and combinations of movements. Give whatever directions or cautions are needed. (If someone decides to twirl, he needs to be careful not to make himself dizzy. Twirling once every so often is enough. Children could dance with partners, or they could join hands and dance in a group.)

Some of the songs you might know and might feel comfortable to use are suggested below.

"Bicycle Built for Two" (Dacre).
"Blue-Tail Fly" (Southern Folk Song).
"Buffalo Gals" (Traditional Song).
"Down in the Valley" (Kentucky Folk Song).
"Erie Canal" (American Folk Song).
"For He's a Jolly Good Fellow" (Traditional Song).
"I've Been Workin' on the Railroad" (Traditional Song).
"In the Good Old Summertime" (G. Evans).
"Jingle Bells" (J. Pierpont).
"Joshua Fit the Battle of Jericho" (Spiritual).
"The More We Get Together" (Old German Melody).
"Oh, What a Beautiful Mornin'" from "Oklahoma."
"Old Dan Tucker" (D. Emmett).
"On Top of Old Smokey" (Kentucky Folk Song).
"Pop Goes the Weasel" (Traditional Song).
"Red River Valley" (American Cowboy Song).
"Rig-a-Jig-Jig" (English Folk Song).
"Roll On, Columbia" (Woody Guthrie).
"Sidewalks of New York" (J. Blake).
"Skip to My Lou" (American Folk Song).
"Sur Le Pont d'Avignon" (French Folk Song).
"When Johnny Comes Marching Home" (Lambert).

Part Two

LESSONS IN

HARMONIC SINGING

Most people would agree that when harmony is added to a song, the melody sounds more attractive. This process in music is like putting shading and other detail on a line drawing. The lines give the viewer the idea; the shadings make the lines stand out and give the picture clarity. A melody in music makes a statement; with harmony surrounding it, that melody appears more important.

In this section we will be describing ways in which a teacher can lead children to sing harmony together. If you are a person who worries about your ability to carry a tune, let alone sing in harmony, these chapters will show you some surprisingly easy ways of leading children in harmonic singing. Did you know there are songs which harmonize when sung together? With the assistance of a few capable or musically talented children, rounds can easily be sung under your guidance.

To introduce children to the study of harmony you will be using a kind of step-by-step procedure that was followed when people first decided to harmonize music. In ancient times the emphasis was on scales with various intervals between the notes. Composers wrote melodies using different scales for different purposes. It is thought that there could have been harmony used by the orchestras of Egypt during their Golden Age. But, harmony as we know it had its beginnings in the Middle Ages.

The development of a system of harmonizing was slow and gradual. Undoubtedly people sang in octaves first. Those with high voices would attempt to match the tones of those with low voices and would be singing an octave higher. (Octave tones sound similar to each other because any note an octave higher than another vibrates at exactly twice the frequency.)

It is believed that adding a drone bass to singing was the next step in the development of harmony. The drone is a continuous low tone which has no pattern of rising and falling. We can speculate that monotones who could not distinguish changes in pitch must have been allowed to sing with a choir and that eventually the listeners found the monotonous tones pleasing.

Another accident is probably responsible for the next step in the development of a harmonic system. Those persons who could sing a melody but who had difficulty singing as high as the higher singers, or as low as the lowest, would prefer to sing somewhere in the middle. They would pitch their singing a fourth, or four notes, lower than the high singers. This was a fifth, or five notes, above the low voices. In time, the sounds of these singers did not sound offensive to listeners.

Why does the human ear readily accept the sounds of tones that are a fifth higher than low tones and a fourth lower than those an octave higher? The reason can be found in a natural phenomenon, the arisal of overtones when a tone is sounded. When we hear a clock chime, a violin string vibrate, a voice sing a note, we distinctly hear the tone sounded. We also hear, though only faintly, a number of other tones at higher pitches called overtones. The first overtone is an octave higher than the note sounded. The second overtone is a fifth higher than the octave note. The third overtone is a fourth above that; the fifth is a third higher, etc.

Every time a tone is produced, that tone is accompanied by a number of overtones. If we could watch a string vibrating at the pitch of a low C, we would see that it vibrates not only as a whole, but also in halves. The two halves would produce a tone with twice the number of vibrations, and this would sound an octave higher. The string would also be vibrating in thirds, fourths, and so on, producing vibrations three, four and more times the speed of the fundamental tone. The overtone notes for C would include several higher-pitched C's along with E's and G's. In harmony, a chord with C, E and G is the C major chord. Such a chord is at the basis of the harmony of our times.

In the historical development of harmony we find that descant, a second, less important melody used to accompany the principal melody, developed next. The descant could be in a different rhythm and could use intervals other than fourths, fifths and octaves. The use of descant led to the development of counterpoint, a kind of countermelody which was composed under strict rules.

One kind of counterpoint was the canon. This type of composition is like a round. The first part of the melody is repeated at intervals in either the same or related keys by other voices, and the music of all the voices must sound harmonious when sounded together. From this kind of writing came the round as we know it today. It differs from the canon in that the melody is always repeated in the same key and always at intervals a phrase apart.

The study of harmony can be presented to children almost in the same order in which discoveries were made down the years. You can start with word chants spoken as rounds by groups of children and done in rhythm. Everyone can sing rounds. There are songs that can be sung together; one song would be the principal melody, the other a kind of descant. An ostinato accompaniment (like the drone bass) can be added to a familiar song. Older children can be taught to make chords with their voices and to use the chords to accompany songs.

There is an harmonic music going on around us all the time. Groups of people make it unintentionally when they are together. Take a walk down the halls of your school some time when people are there but classes are not in session. Listen to the tone of the sounds coming from each room; notice how each seems to have its own peculiar tone and how all other new voices tune in to it. Listen to the general tone of the playground. If you listen every day it will always be different as the children seem to "tune in" to each other. At any social gathering people modify their voice tones to create a single sound that is harmonious. It is on experiences like these that the feeling for harmony in music is founded.

Chapter **3**

YOU CAN TEACH ROUNDS

A song like "Are You Sleeping?" or "Row, Row, Row Your Boat" can be sung as a round by almost everyone, even the person whose ability to hold a tune is minimal. The round is a kind of composition that allows people who might otherwise have problems to sing harmony.

It takes effort to sing a round. When young children try it for the first time, they may act challenged, as if singing a round is a contest amongst adversaries who are trying to put the people on the other side off their tune. Beginners at the art may be seen holding their ears to keep out the music of the others, lest they start singing with them and lose their own part. (If your children hold their ears at first, you can ignore them: they will soon abandon the practice.) Children's feelings change quickly from fear to fascination with the pretty harmony that results.

The writing of rounds and canons has challenged composers for centuries. The melody of this kind of composition must have a good rhythm and a pleasing line. At the same time, this melody must sound harmonious when different parts of it are sung together. But, if the music writer is limited by such requirements, singers are less limited since everyone who is to harmonize is privileged to sing the same melodic music. When singing harmony that uses chords, only one part of the singing group sings the melody; the others sing secondary tones that are not pleasing by themselves.

WORD CHANTS AS ROUNDS

Have you ever noticed how often words are spoken in a kind of "round" in real life situations? For example, what would happen if a large group of people was trying to hear a speaker but some members of the group were too far away? We would find that those who were nearest would be continuously relaying the message to those at the back. In other situations people keep passing a place where the same words are said again and again; each person or group hears the words in turn. People passing a newsboy who is shouting: "Read all about it!" and reciting the headlines would make a round by chanting the headlines as the boy repeated his recitation.

The word chants in the following pages describe and dramatize a few such actual occurrences. If the children are to do them successfully as rounds, it is important for them to learn them in strict rhythm. In the text, note values have been placed over every syllable, and words have been grouped into measures in the way that they would be if the music were melodic. The underlying beats are indicated by the numbers placed over the notes.

The first step in presenting a word chant is to write the words with divisions into syllables on the chalk board. Leave a wide space between the lines. Next, draw the notes and rests over the words and syllables and draw measure bars. Finally, write the numbers over the notes.

Have the children read the words. Make sure they understand their meanings and can pronounce all of them correctly. If they have difficulty changing from notes of one rhythm to notes of another, have everyone clap them while you are counting the beats of the measures. (Older children may be able to count and clap at the same time.)

When they are ready, the children should read the words in rhythm. They should watch each syllable and the note above it at the same time. If they are skeptical about their ability to do this, tell them: "With part of your eye you will see the word or syllable, and with another part of your eye you will see the note that tells you how fast to go." If necessary, you should tap or clap a steady beat while the words are read in rhythm. (In at least one of the following chants the children will keep the beat.)

The Roman numerals in the word chant indicate how many groups are recommended to do the chant as a round. It is advisable when more than two divisions are suggested that the round be tried first with two parts. When that has been done well, have three parts, then four. The first group starts. The moment they get to Roman numeral "II" the second group starts. As soon as the first group reaches Roman numeral "III" and the second group reaches "II," the third group is to start, and so forth.

GIANTS AND DRAGONS   (Grades 1-3)

The children should use normal voices until they say the words of the giants and dragons or make their sounds. They will enjoy using their deepest voices in these places. The chant will be recited by two groups. It can be done at least twice. (In music these are repeat signs: |: :|)

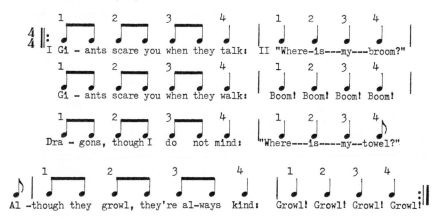

THE BARNYARD   (Grades 1-3)

There are two sections to this chant. The introduction is to be recited by all voices. The round can be done in two, three, or four parts, and it should be repeated. If the children have problems changing from fast to slower rhythms, they can let their hands "count" for them. Encourage them to pat softly on their thighs (or desk tops) in a steady beat as much as needed.

Introduction (to be spoken in unison):

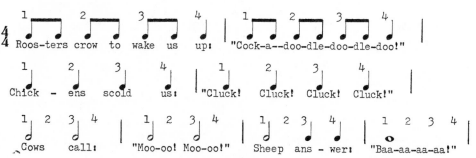

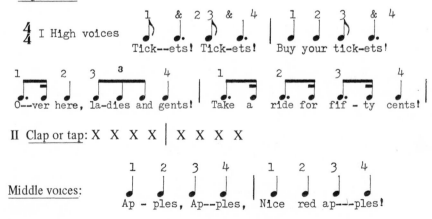

I Cock-a-doo--dle-doo-dle-doo, II Cluck! Cluck! Cluck! Cluck!

III Moo - oo!   Moo - oo!   IV Baa - aa - aa - aa!

THE CARNIVAL   (Grades 3-6)

This chant is to be spoken by two groups. They should imagine they are walking around at a carnival, one group following the other. As each approaches a booth or an event, it imitates the vendor, speaking his words in the voice pitch he uses when giving his sales talk. (So the children will have no problem with remembering pitches, we suggest the first vendor be high-pitched, the next at a middle level, the third low, the fourth high, etc.) Children will naturally say each sales talk in a rising and falling singsong at the pitch level. To get from one vendor to another the carnival goers take exactly eight steps. The sounds of walking should barely be heard; they should be made by lightly clapping the hands or tapping a pencil on a desk, on the floor, etc.

If the children wish to act it out, various ones could act as the vendors—selling tickets to each event or selling apples, popcorn, lollipops, balloons, etc. Individuals would be seen taking chances, proving their skill, buying food and other goodies. The children could add other amusements and create more stanzas. They could have more than two groups of carnival goers.

I <u>High voices</u>:

I High voices   Tick--ets! Tick-ets!   Buy your tick-ets!

O--ver here, la-dies and gents!   Take a ride for fif - ty cents!

II <u>Clap or tap</u>: X X X X | X X X X

<u>Middle voices</u>:   Ap - ples, Ap--ples,   Nice red ap---ples!

One will cost you just a dime; Buy them while there still is time!

Clap or tap: X X X X | X X X X

Low voices:

Here you are, step right up; Get the ball in the cup.

Aim it right; win a prize. La - dies, it's good ex-er - cise!

Clap or tap: X X X X | X X X X

High voices:

Pop corn! Pop corn! Hot but--tered pop corn!

Buy some pop corn! Hot but-tered pop corn!

Clap or tap: X X X X | X X X X

Middle voices:

How a--bout a nice bal-loon? A - ny co-lor of bal-loon!

Get one now; they're go-ing fast; No - one knows how long they'll last!

Clap or tap: X X X X | X X X X

Low voices:

Lol - li--pops on a stick; A - ny fla - vor, take your pick!

Red, yel - low, e - ven blue; Buy one; buy two!

Clap or tap: X X X X | X X X X

High voices:

1 2 3 4   1 2 3 4
Hey, there, folks,you can win;   Bet a num - ber, then I spin.

1 2 3 4   1 2 3 4
Take a chance; have some fun; Here's a game for ev' - ry - one.
Clap or tap: X X X X | X X X X

1 2 3 4   1 2 3 4
Middle voices: (slowly) Le - mon-ade!   Le, - mon-ade!

1 2 3 4   1 2 3 4
Nice   cool   Le - mon-ade!
Clap or tap: X X X X | X X X X

Low voices:

1 2 3 4   1 2 3 4
Dime a shot..Hit the clown.. Test your skill..Knock 'im down!

1 2 3 4   1 2 3 4
Girls and boys, don't be shy; You can hit 'im if you try!
Clap or tap: X X X X | X X X X

1 2 3 4   1 2 3 4
Normal voices: What's this? We're through? It can't be true!

1 2 3 4   1 2 3 4
Let's rest, and then,   We'll go a-gain!

THE FIRE   (Grades 3-6)

This is the story of the fire in Shepherd's Valley. Someone living on one side of the valley sees it first and telephones the fire department in his town. Then someone on the other side sees it and calls the fire department in his town. The first engines rush to the scene; moments later the second engines are on their way. Together the firemen rescue the people and put out the fire.

Everyone takes all the parts in the story—the ringing phone, the fireman who answers, the excited caller, the bell on the fire truck, the siren, the other firemen, the trapped victims, and the onlookers. The speakers should pitch their voices appropriately and should show suitable excitement.

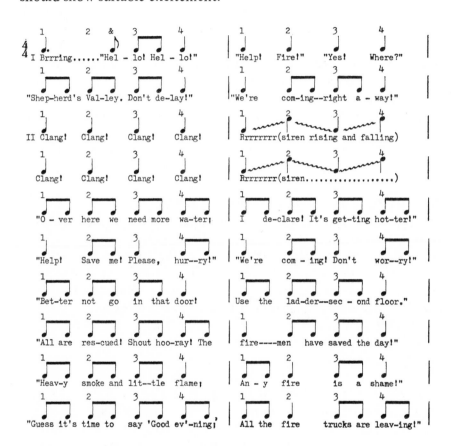

PRESENTING ROUNDS AND CANONS

The rounds and canons that follow have been chosen either because they are familiar to most people or they are easy to figure out. Songs like "Are You Sleeping?," "Three Blind Mice," and "Row, Row, Row Your Boat" are generally sung by people all their lives. They are easy enough for first-grade children to sing and at the same time are sufficiently interesting to the more sophisticated sixth graders. Such songs can be presented without hesitation.

The songs that are unfamiliar can be worked out in various ways. You can figure them out by yourself and present them to your children by rote. Or, if the children are at second-grade level or higher, you could put the words and music on the chalkboard to be worked out by you and the children together. See pages 92 and 93 for the first steps in reading words in rhythm. See Chapter I if you are uncertain of any time values for notes.

As soon as the children have learned to read the words of the song in rhythm, they are ready to figure out the note names of the music. The scale name of the starting note is given at the beginning of each song. Sound the pitch of the first note on a pitch pipe, piano or other melody instrument, and tell the children to sing the notes of the first phrase to themselves. They should go over them at least once silently. When this has been done, have the notes of the phrase sung out loud. Follow the same procedure for each phrase. Finally, have the whole song sung with notes.

For the next step, have the children hum the melody or sing the notes on a neutral syllable such as "la." If they have problems staying together, point to each note to be sung. If there are problems with keeping the proper rhythm, you can tap a steady beat as you point to the notes. As a final step, the children will sing the words.

It is extremely important when singing rounds and canons that the singers give each note and each rest the exact amount of time specified in the notation so that singing such a song in parts will be successful. The song should be well known and memorized, if possible, so that there will be no hesitation when sung in harmony.

You can easily differentiate between the rounds and the canons. A round is composed so that singers of the different parts come in a phrase apart. Every phrase blends harmonically with every other. A canon has a different spacing of parts. The second part is sometimes sung in a different (related) key. This part is usually brought in soon after the song has started, not by phrase.

Look for the Roman numerals in the song you have learned. If numeral "II" and higher numbers are less than a phrase apart, the song is a canon; if they are a phrase apart, it is a round. When the song is sung in parts, it will be started by one group who will sing up to numeral "II." At that point you will signal the second group to come in. When the first singers reach numeral "III," you will signal the third group to start, and so forth.

On the day that the children are finally to sing the new song in parts, have them review it in unison. Next, divide the class into two sections, one section to your left, the other to your right. Ask each group to sing the song alone. If one side sounds weaker than the other, either in volume or in its ability to hold the tune or keep the rhythm, move one or more singers from the stronger side to the weaker until the two groups are balanced.

Sing the song as a round or canon. If the first attempt goes well, ask the children to sing the song again, going through it twice. The moment each group has finished, they should start over.

First and second-grade children are usually limited to only singing rounds and to singing these in just two parts. Older and more capable children will be able to sing rounds in three parts or more, whatever the song requires. Divide the children into the number of groups called for, and test them for evenness in ability and volume. Be sure the groups are ranged in front of you in such a way that you can easily signal each one to begin singing.

Grade levels at which each song can most readily be performed have been suggested. However, you should not hesitate to ask older children to try to do an expert job of singing some of the songs that have been recommended for lower grades. Nor should you feel deterred from asking capable young children to try some of the songs that have been designated as most suitable for older children. Probably third and fourth graders will be able to sing almost all of the rounds and canons and will do it with enjoyment.

All of the songs can be accompanied with melody instruments, and some could be enhanced with an accompaniment by rhythm instruments. Children who can read music or those who can find tunes by ear may be able to play the music on piano, xylophone, resonator bells or any other melody instrument you might have in the classroom. Children who are studying flute, violin or some other orchestral instrument could play along with the singing or could play the music alone as an introduction. They could play a coda at the end, an interlude in the middle, etc. If rhythm instruments are used, they should be chosen carefully; they can be used to keep a steady underlying beat.

Some rounds and canons can be dramatized. With some of the songs it would be appropriate to do motions. And for many of them a dance could be created. Everyone might do the dance while singing, or a chosen few might be the dancers, everyone else the singers.

THE ROUNDS AND CANONS

DOWN BY THE STATION   (Grades 1-4)

This song can be dramatized. Some children can be the puffer billies. These are the little engines that are seen in railroad yards where they shuttle back and forth lining up the cars of a train or moving them from place to place. Other children will be the train cars being pulled by the puffer billies. Driving each little engine is someone who "turns the little handle."

Rhythm instruments can make some of the sounds of the railroad yard. A triangle or bell might be heard occasionally. Sand blocks could make the swishing sounds of the chugging trains. Rhythm sticks can tap like wheels clicking on the rails.

DOWN BY THE STATION

Traditional Round

I
do
Down   by   the   sta - tion,   ear-ly   in   the   morn - ing,

II
See the lit-tle   puf-fer bil-lies   all   in   a   row.

III
See the lit-tle   driv - er   turn   the lit-tle   han - dle,

IV
Puff!   Puff!   Choo!   Choo!   Off   they   go!

LITTLE TOM TINKER   (Grades 1-4)

The children will enjoy making their voices slide on "Ma! Ma!" so that they sound like someone who is distressed and in pain.

LITTLE TOM TINKER

Traditional Round

TICK TOCK   (Grades 1-4)

Rhythm instruments can effectively be added to the singing of this song. Discuss the words with the children. Have any of them seen a clock that stands on the floor; have they noticed how slowly the pendulum swings? What instrument makes sounds like a ticking floor clock? (The wood block is a good choice.) Smaller clocks that might stand on shelves or hang on the wall can be imitated by tapping pencils or rhythm sticks. And the sounds of little watches can be simulated on such instruments as the triangle or finger cymbals.

Instruments should be played only during unison singing or each should follow one part, coming in when the words indicate. The instrument representing the big clock would start and would play half notes throughout; the second instrument would come in at "II" and would play in quarter notes; the third instrument would play eighth notes starting at "III."

TICK TOCK

Words adapted   Traditional Round

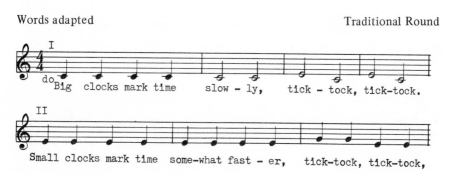

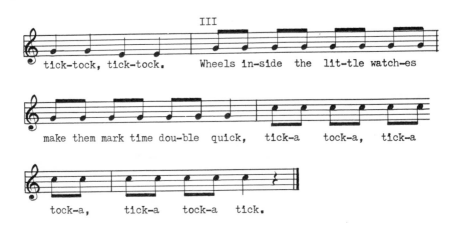

RABBIT BOLD   (Grades 1-4)

Train the children to wait three beats at the end of the song before they start it again.

Let the children briefly dramatize this song. They might act the part of the gardener with one child as the bold rabbit eating carrots. Everyone would point a finger while talking to him. At the end they might throw up their hands and scare the rabbit off.

RABBIT BOLD

J.L.R.   From a tune of Smetana

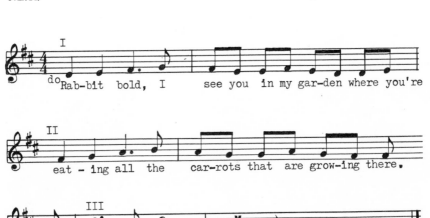

WHY SHOULDN'T MY GOOSE?   (Grades 1-4)

There is an extraordinarily wide range of tones in this song. The lowest, middle C, is in the first phrase; the highest, F, is in the third. So that the children's voices can reach both the lowest and the highest notes it is important to make low F the starting pitch.

WHY SHOULDN'T MY GOOSE?

Traditional Round

Why should-n't my goose Lay as well as thy goose,
When I paid for my goose Twice as much as yours?

THE BELL (LA CLOCHE)   (Grades 1-4)

Use a resonator bell to accompany the singing. (If you have no bells, use piano, xylophone or other melody instrument.) The tones of the first and last phrases can be played throughout.

THE BELL
(LA CLOCHE)

J.L.R.   French Round

Ding, dong,   ding, dong,   'Tis the bell of   ear-ly morn
Din, don,   din, don,   C'est la clo-che   du ma-tin,

Which rings out to greet the dawn: Good-day, good-day!
Qui sonne au le - ver du jour: Bon-jour, bon-jour!

ARE YOU SLEEPING?   (Grades 1-6)

Even the youngest children can learn to sing the words of this song in French and will be proud that they can do it. There are many ways to accompany this song on instruments. A drum might play the rhythm of the last phrase throughout, or a melody instrument like a xylophone or piano could repeatedly play the notes. Older children will be able to play the whole song on a melody instrument. Have someone play an introduction that has been created by the children.

ARE YOU SLEEPING?
(FRÈRE JACQUES)

Traditional

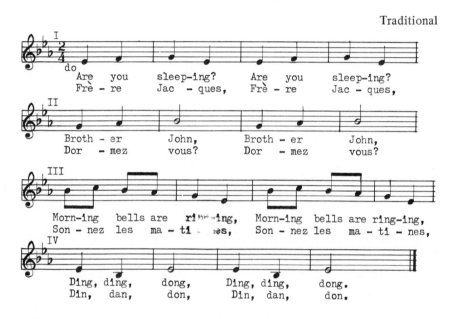

THREE BLIND MICE   (Grades 1-6)

The music and the events of this song move so quickly as to make dramatization difficult. It would also be hard for anyone to play the whole melody on a melody instrument. However, the notes of the first phrase can be used for an introduction and an accompaniment for the whole song. After the children have learned this song and ARE YOU SLEEPING? suggest that they sing them simultaneously. (Both songs have been written in the same key for the purpose of singing them together.) To do this, divide the children into two groups. Have one group start one song; after the first phrase has been sung, the second group starts the second song. When the first group finishes the first song, it sings the second, and when the second group finishes its song, it sings the first song. If they are ambitious enough, a large group of capable children can be divided into eight sections in order to sing the two songs as an eight-part round.

THREE BLIND MICE

Old Round

Three blind mice, Three blind mice, See how they run, See how they run, They all ran af-ter the farm-er's wife, She cut off their tails with a carv-ing knife, did you ev-er see such a sight in your life, As three blind mice?

ROW, ROW, ROW YOUR BOAT   (Grades 1-6)

Make sure that no one slows down when singing the third phrase. Young children may sing the song as a two-part round; older children may do it in three or four parts.

All the children can do motions while singing. They should bend forward and pretend to grasp an oar in each hand. Then, keeping time with the music, they would pull back on the oars.

ROW, ROW, ROW YOUR BOAT

Traditional Round

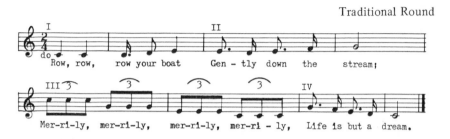

Row, row, row your boat Gen - tly down the stream;

Mer-ri-ly, mer-ri-ly, mer-ri-ly, mer-ri - ly, Life is but a dream.

SCOTLAND'S BURNING   (Grades 1-6)

The tune of the first phrase is the same as that of the fourth. The song can be sung by younger children as a two-part round, by older children as a three- or four-part round. Ask them to think of motions to accompany the singing.

SCOTLAND'S BURNING

Traditional Round

Scot-land's burn-ing, Scot-land's burn - ing, Look out,

Look out! Fire! Fire! Fire! Fire! Pour on wa-ter, Pour on wa - ter.

FROGS   (Grades 1-6)

Show the children how to make the last phrase of this song sound like one continuous sound. They should hold "Brr-" for almost a full two beats, then slide their voices up to the last note.

FROGS

Traditional Round

Hear the live-ly song of the frogs in yon-der pond:

Krik,   krik,   krik, krik, krik, krik, Brrr - oom!

SWEETLY SINGS THE DONKEY   (Grades 1-6)

Ask a small group of singers to sing the third phrase twice through as an introduction to the song. They might continue singing while the others sing the song in unison. Then have it sung as a round.

SWEETLY SINGS THE DONKEY

English Round

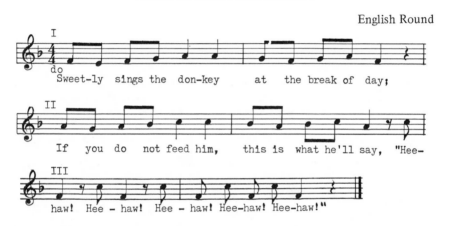

do
Sweet-ly sings the don-key   at   the break of day;

If   you do   not feed him,   this is what he'll say, "Hee-

haw! Hee - haw! Hee - haw! Hee-haw! Hee-haw!"

KOOKABURRA   (Grades 1-6)

The kookaburra is an Australian bird that looks like a kingfisher, with a crested head and a short tail. Its call sounds like a coarse laugh. The bird of the song is called "king of the bush;" in Australia the bush is a thick, uncleared forest.

The song is appealing when sung in unison. Young children will be able to sing it in two parts; older children can try it in three or four parts.

KOOKABURRA

M. Sinclair   Australian Round

so
Koo-ka-bur - ra sits on an   old gum tree,

FOR HEALTH AND STRENGTH   (Grades 1-6)

This song of thanks is a universal favorite which sounds effective when sung either in unison or as a round.

FOR HEALTH AND STRENGTH

Traditional Round

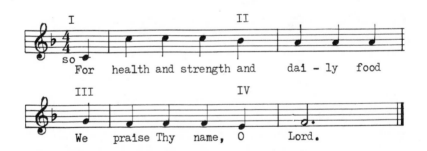

STREET CRIES   (Grades 2-6)

Many of today's children do not realize that it is possible for vendors to sell goods and services in the streets. Not too many years ago, it was a common occurrence to have tradesmen pushing little carts or riding in horse-drawn carts and calling out their wares to the residents of the street. Children should be encouraged to use strong voices when they sing this song.

STREET CRIES

Traditional Round

so Chairs to mend, old chairs to mend, Mack-er-el, fresh mack - er - el; Old rags, an - y old rags?

HALLOWEEN   (Grades 2-6)

A banshee is a spirit in Irish folklore that supposedly makes wailing sounds. Two or three children could wail and moan while the others were singing the song. On the word "cry," voices should slide from high C to middle C. The music of the song will sound spooky because it is in the minor mode.

HALLOWEEN

J.L.R.   J.L.R.

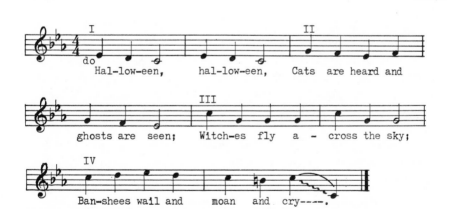

do Hal-low-een, hal-low-een, Cats are heard and ghosts are seen; Witch-es fly a - cross the sky; Ban-shees wail and moan and cry----.

THE BROOM (DE BEZEM)   (Grades 2-6)

There are many ways to sing this song. The first two phrases are sung by a questioner; the last two by the person who answers.

There could be a singer and an echo group on each phrase, since the words are always sung twice. And the song can be sung as a round in two, three or four parts.

The children can sing the Dutch words: De bezem = de bayzem; Wat doe je er mee = vaht doo yah air may; Wij vegen er mee = way faygen air may; De vloer aan = de fluhr ahn.

THE BROOM
(DE BEZEM)

J.L.R.   Dutch Round

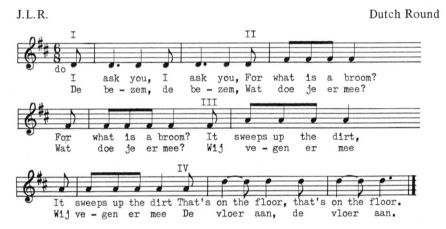

SING, SING TOGETHER   (Grades 2-6)

The time signature of this song is 6/8. Think of the time as being two beats to a measure. A dotted quarter note (♩.) would get one beat and so would a quarter and eighth (♩ ♪) and three eighth notes (♫♪). A dotted half note (♩.) would get two beats.

SING, SING TOGETHER

Old English Round

LOVELY EVENING   (Grades 3-6)

The melody of this song is easy to sing, but younger children find it difficult because they tend to sing the sustained notes too quickly.

The singing can be accompanied by someone playing the F's of the last phrase on resonator bells, xylophone or piano. Two F's, a low one and a high one, will give the effect of evening bells ringing. Someone should be able to find the whole melody on an instrument. If the song is sung in three parts, there should be an instrumental accompanist for each part.

LOVELY EVENING

Old Round

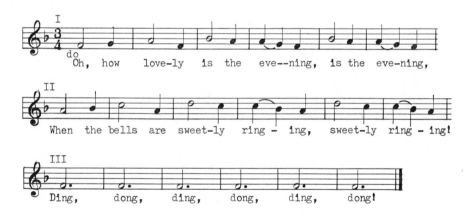

WHITE CORAL BELLS   (Grades 3-6)

The stalks of coral bells reach two or three feet. Each has several flowerets. Lily-of-the-valley is a plant which has multiple flowers that hang down like little white bells. They have a sweet fragrance.

Both the rhythm and the melody of the song are deceptively difficult and must be mastered before the song is tried as a round.

WHITE CORAL BELLS

Old English Round

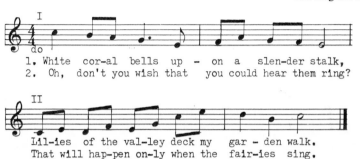

GOOD NIGHT TO YOU ALL   (Grades 3-6)

The song should be sung softly and with sustained tones. The notes of the last phrase can be played on a melody instrument as an introduction or as a simple accompaniment to the song.

GOOD NIGHT TO YOU ALL

Traditional Round

UPWARD TRAIL   (Grades 3-6)

Hikers enjoy singing this song as they walk. It is easily sung as a canon. Notice that the second group of singers comes in on the second measure as if to echo the first group while those singers are holding "trail."

UPWARD TRAIL

Traditional Canon

We're on the up-ward trail, We're on the up-ward trail,

Sing--ing, sing-ing, Ev'-ry-bod - y sing-ing, As we go. Home-ward bound.

LEAVIN' OLD TEXAS   (Grades 3-6)

Suggest that someone play an instrument that makes sounds like the clip-clop of horses' hoofs during the singing of the song.

The song is really a canon. The second group of singers enters after the first group has sung the first four words and sounds like an echo of the first.

LEAVIN' OLD TEXAS

Cowboy Song

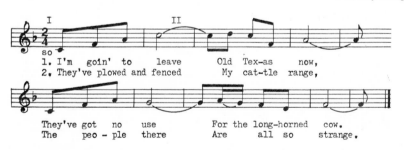

1. I'm goin' to leave Old Tex-as now,
2. They've plowed and fenced My cat-tle range,

They've got no use For the long-horned cow.
The peo - ple there Are all so strange.

COME, DANCE (ZUM TANZ)   (Grades 3-6)

The two phrases of this canon are identical except for the last measures. When the song is sung as a canon, it will sound as if the second part is pursuing the first as the melody moves down, then up, and then down the scale.

If they are interested, have the children learn to sing the German words. They should make up a dance to perform while singing.

COME, DANCE
(ZUM TANZ)

J.L.R.   German Canon

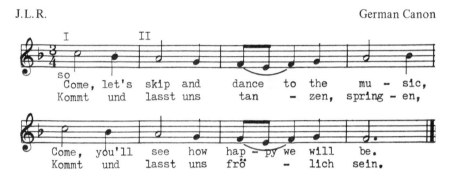

Come, let's skip and   dance   to the   mu - sic,
Kommt   und   lasst uns   tan - zen, spring - en,

Come,   you'll   see   how   hap - py   we   will   be.
Kommt   und   lasst uns   frö - lich   sein.

SIGNS OF SPRING   (Grades 3-6)

The melody of this song is reminiscent of the first theme in "Country Gardens" by Percy Grainger, a composition most familiar to beginning piano students. The music of the first and third phrases is the same; that of the second and fourth phrases is the same except for the last two notes. Suggest to the children that they create a dance for the music.

SIGNS OF SPRING

J.L.R.   Old English Folk Tune

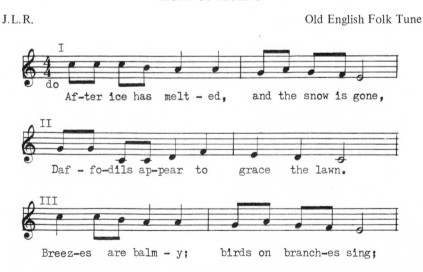

do
Af-ter ice has melt - ed,   and the snow is gone,

Daf - fo-dils ap-pear to   grace   the lawn.

Breez-es   are balm - y;   birds on branch-es sing;

These are the signs that it is spring.

MUSIC ALONE SHALL LIVE   (Grades 3-6)

Discuss the meaning of the words. The children may think that because music exists only while it is being performed, it is not permanent. Arts like painting and architecture seem more permanent; at least they are tangible and can be seen. But they wear out in time or can be destroyed; music can always be recalled.

MUSIC ALONE SHALL LIVE

German Round

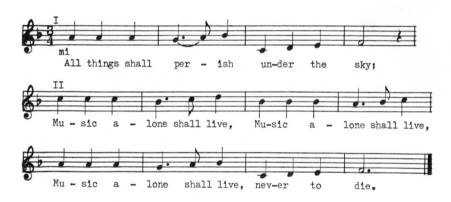

All things shall per - ish un-der the sky;

Mu - sic a - lone shall live, Mu-sic a - lone shall live,

Mu - sic a - lone shall live, nev-er to die.

MERRILY, MERRILY   (Grades 3-6)

This cheerful melody is reminiscent of a tune played by a hunting horn, and the rhythm of the song reminds one of the galloping of horses during a hunt. The children might enjoy acting it out. Someone could pretend to be sounding the horn; others could gallop as in a chase.

MERRILY, MERRILY

Old English Round

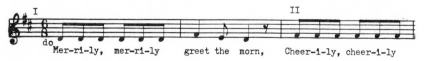

Mer-ri-ly, mer-ri-ly   greet the morn,   Cheer-i-ly, cheer-i-ly

sound the horn,   Hark to the ech-oes,   hear them play O'er

hill and dale and   far a - way.

CHRISTMAS IS COMING   (Grades 3-6)

The old man of the song begs for money at Christmas-time. In the England of those days a person could buy food and drink for just a few pennies. The English penny was worth more than the American penny. See if the children can guess that a "ha'-penny" (pronounced HAY-penny) is a half penny.

CHRISTMAS IS COMING

English Round

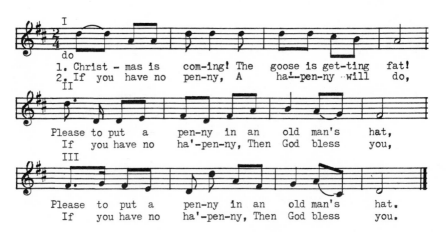

1. Christ - mas is   com-ing! The   goose is get-ting   fat!
2. If you have no   pen-ny, A   ha'-pen-ny will   do,

Please to put a   pen-ny in an   old man's   hat,
If you have no   ha'-pen-ny, Then God bless   you,

Please to put a   pen-ny in an   old man's   hat.
If you have no   ha'-pen-ny, Then God bless   you.

THE BELL DOTH TOLL   (Grades 4-6)

When a bell tolls, it rings very slowly. Every word and syllable should be sustained for the full amount of time indicated in the notes of the song. Someone could play the bell sounds of the third phrase on a resonant melody instrument like a resonator bell.

THE BELL DOTH TOLL

Old English Round

THE SCALE   (Grades 4-6)

The time signature for this song is a capital "C" with a vertical line through it. This tells the performer to sing in "cut time," twice as fast as usual. The music is not as easy as it probably looks. It can be learned at a slower speed and eventually sung at a fast tempo.

THE SCALE

Beethoven

Mi fa so la ti do re   mi,   mi re do ti la so fa   mi.

COME, FOLLOW   (Grades 4-6)

Every phrase of this song is different in melody and in rhythm. Singers must know it perfectly before attempting to sing it as a round. It is well worth the extra time and effort needed to sing this music, and the children will appreciate its high quality and elegance.

COME, FOLLOW

Old English Round

do
Come, fol-low, fol-low, fol-low, Fol-low, fol-low,

fol-low me. Whi-ther shall I fol-low, fol-low, fol-low,

Whi-ther shall I fol-low,   fol-low thee? To the green-wood,

to the green-wood, To   the green-wood, green-wood tree.

HEY, HO! NOBODY HOME   (Grades 4-6)

The music of this song is in the minor mode. No one is certain of the origin of the song. Perhaps Christmas carolers composed it while walking away from an empty house. At any rate, the singers are begging as they go from door to door. The children could make up a pantomime about what happens.

When the melody is played on a piano, one black note, B^b, must be used. All the other notes used will be white. Encourage a few children to learn to play it. Then assign them to play in different areas of the piano keyboard so that they can play the song as a round. The first phrase music makes a good introduction to the song.

HEY, HO! NOBODY HOME

Old English Round

TALLIS' CANON   (Grades 4-6)

This is one of the oldest hymn tunes still being used. The music was written by Thomas Tallis in 1507. Thomas Ken wrote the words in 1709.

The song can be sung as either a canon or a round. Roman numerals without parentheses indicate the places the two groups should start if it is to be sung as a canon. Numbers in parenthesis indicate the beginnings of phrases and should be followed if the song is to be sung as a round.

TALLIS' CANON

Thomas Ken   Thomas Tallis

DONA NOBIS PACEM   (Grades 4-6)

The Latin words pray: "Give us peace." The music of this old round is difficult, but you and your children will find it so beautiful and appealing, you will feel it worth your while to figure it out. It will not be beyond the capabilities of fifth and sixth graders as well as the abler fourth-grade children to sing as a round.

DONA NOBIS PACEM

Traditional Round

Chapter **4**

YOU CAN TEACH PART SINGING

The chapter on teaching rounds showed you a relatively easy way to lead children in part singing. Rounds and canons are contrapuntal because the harmony is made when two or more melodies, each with its own peculiar rhythm, are sounded together. In this chapter, you will be shown another easy way to have children sing contrapuntally, using a second song for a descant.

The term "part singing" implies that the melody of a song is accompanied by one or more secondary parts which are less interesting than the melody itself and that could not be sung alone; their only function is to accompany the melody. In this chapter, you will find out how to have children sing parts with their melodies that will enhance the sound but which can be done with a minimum of effort.

For instance, there are songs which can be accompanied with as few as two different notes sung repeatedly. There are songs which can be accompanied with an ostinato of a few notes, a single phrase that sounds well when sung over and over with the melody. It can be easy to harmonize the last few notes of a song. Groups of older or more capable singers will be able to make chords with their voices to accompany a melody.

Every school child learns early that not all notes make harmony when sounded together. Discord arises when two or more inharmonic notes are sounded and their overtones clash.

Not all discord is displeasing, and in recent years various composers have written music with dissonant harmonies that people have found exciting and appealing. One of them was Charles Ives, an American composer of the early twentieth century, who got many of his ideas for composition from his father. George Ives was a musician who invited people to sing in his choirs, even if they could not sing in tune. He felt that their enthusiasm was all that really mattered, and he was not bothered by the droning of singers who were off key. His son, the composer, felt similarly and deliberately wrote music that was dissonant. He would combine two songs or pieces of music which had different harmonies and different rhythms, and he would get interesting results.

Since it takes an expert to make satisfying combinations of dissonant harmonies, it is not recommended that you allow your children to make a lot of off-key harmony. On the other hand, you should not dampen the enthusiasm of imperfect singers; it takes most people a while to get the knack of making harmony.

Teaching Part Singing with This Book

You will find grade levels suggested for presenting the lessons in harmonizing songs. These are intended only to guide you in choosing work for your class. If, for instance, you have young children or children with limited ability, they may not be able to participate in many of the activities of this chapter. First-and-second-grade children may be so busy just learning to sing, they may have little or no awareness or appreciation of harmony and little or no ability to sing in parts.

On the other hand, if you have one or more strong singers in your group, you will find that they can lead the whole class. With their help you should be able to present some of the rounds and canons of the previous chapter as well as some of the song combinations in which one song is used as descant in this chapter. Younger children will also be able to sing a simple ostinato to other songs.

If you have the ability to sing harmony, let your strong singers help the class sing the melody while you sing the harmony part alone. But at all times, keep in mind this general rule: it is best not to attempt harmony with children unless, and until, there is a good chance they can do it successfully.

To seat a group of between twenty and thirty children for part singing, have them make two or three rows from front to back. Strong singers should be behind those with less ability. Make as many divisions as needed from left to right in front of you. There should be blocks of singers grouped together on each part.

Everyone will have an equal chance to learn to sing in harmony; this means that parts will frequently be reversed. There should be no distinction in parts unless there are boys whose voices are changing; such boys should be assigned to sing in the range in which they are most comfortable.

If necessary, assure your singers that the parts they are asked to sing will be pitched neither too high nor too low for their voices. Parts should not be named "soprano," "alto," etc.; instead, they should be called "melody," "descant," "ostinato," "harmony part," or "chord parts." Usually there will be three chord parts, and they should be called "high," "middle," or "low." Singing in parts should be done lightly, without strain.

As soon as you have made divisions of the singers, test each section for balance in volume. Next, test the sections for ability to hold a part by having each one sing a short phrase of harmony while everyone else sings melody. As soon as you think you have a well-functioning arrangement, make it permanent; it will be changed only if members are absent, if voices change, etc.

Throughout this chapter you will find capital letters printed over words in the songs. These are chord names. A chordal accompaniment can be played on piano, Autoharp, guitar, etc. In a few cases a song can be accompanied by a single chord; in many cases a song can be accompanied by only two different chords; and in most cases it takes just three chords to accompany the songs.

Not only can chords be played on instruments to enrich the sounds of the music. A melody instrument like the piano, xylophone, a set of resonator bells, etc., can be played to assist the singers of the harmony parts. The starting note of each part is given in the text in both letter and syllable names, and the rest of the notes are written in syllables.

Whenever a vocal group sings harmony, a means for having each part start on its particular pitch is needed. It is customary to have the singers on each part hum the starting pitch and hold it while the other parts join in. This may take several seconds, and sometimes singers run out of breath. Since there are always a few people on each part in a class of children, it is possible to keep a tone going indefinitely if each person quietly takes a breath whenever he has the need. In other words, it is unlikely that all of the people on a part would need to breathe at the same moment.

Give the singers on the lowest part their pitch first, then those on the middle part, and the ones on the highest part last. Have the notes hummed lightly and listen for blend and balance. Your hand (or hands) should be up in front of you; when everyone is ready, drop your hand as a signal for the humming to stop. Immediately raise your hand to signal the singing to begin.

USING SONGS AS DESCANTS

A descant is a counter melody which harmonizes with, and is used to accompany, a principal melody. The notes of a descant are often, though not necessarily, pitched higher than those of the melody. The word *descant* derives from the Latin "dis," meaning "apart," and "cantus," meaning "song." A "song apart" may be sung by a small number of voices, or it may be sung with a group equal in volume to the melody singers.

The descants in the following section are familiar songs which have been chosen to accompany other well-known songs. A pair of songs must be of equal length and similar character, and they must be harmonized by the same sequence of chords if the match is to be successful. Accompaniment by piano, Autoharp or guitar can be added by following the letters for the chords which are written over the words.

All of the singers should be able to sing both songs and sing them with assurance. They should be divided into two equal groups (or the descant may sound muted). Each group should sing its part alone before they sing the parts together. Give the pitch to the singers of the lower part. While they hum it, give the pitch to the upper part. Drop your hand to signal the humming to stop. Raise it to signal the singing to begin.

Songs with Descants

Song: THE FARMER IN THE DELL   **First note**: middle C   Grades 1-3

Descant: ROW, ROW, ROW YOUR BOAT   **First note**: F

```
        F           F          │F               F
1. The farmer in the dell—,  The│farmer in    the dell—,
        Row,  row,  row your boat,│Gently down the stream,


        F               F          │F             F
   Heigh - ho,  the  derry - o  The│farm-er in  the dell.
   Merrily, merrily,  merrily, merrily,│Life  is but a   dream.
```

2. The farmer takes a wife . . . . .
3. The wife takes a child . . . . .
4. The child takes a dog . . . . .
5. The dog takes a cat . . . . .
6. The cat takes the mouse . . . . .
7. The mouse takes the cheese . . . . .
8. The cheese stands alone . . . . .

Song: SKIP TO MY LOU   **First note**: A   Grades 2-4

Descant: JOHN BROWN HAD A LITTLE INDIAN   **First note**: F

1 F F	F F
1. Flies in the buttermilk,	shoo, fly, shoo!
John Brown	had a little Indian,

C_7 C_7	C_7 C_7
Flies in the buttermilk,	shoo, fly, shoo!
John Brown	had a little Indian,

F F	F F
Flies in the buttermilk,	shoo, fly, shoo!
John Brown	had a little Indian,

C_7 C_7	F F
Skip to my Lou, my	dar - ling.
One lit-tle Indi-an	boy.

2. Little red wagon, painted blue . . . . .
3. Lost my partner, what'll I do? . . . . .
4. I'll find another one prettier than you . . . . .

Song: GO TELL AUNT RHODIE   **First note**: A   Grades 2-4

Descant: LONDON BRIDGE   **First note**: high C

F	F	C_7	F
1. Go tell Aunt	Rho - die,	Go tell Aunt	Rho - die,
London bridge is	falling down,	falling down,	falling down,

F	F	C_7	F
Go tell Aunt	Rho - die, Her	old gray goose is	dead.
London bridge is	falling down,	My fair	lady.

2. The one she'd been saving . . . . . To make a feather bed.
3. She died in the mill pond . . . . . Standing on her head.
4. The goslings are crying . . . . . The old gray goose is dead.
5. The gander is weeping . . . . . The old gray goose is dead.

Song: EENCY WEENCY SPIDER   **First note:** C   Grades 2-4

Descant: DOWN BY THE STATION   **First note:** F

F F	C₇ F
An	eency weency spi-der went	up the wa-ter spout,
	Down by the sta-tion	early in the morn-ing,

F   F   C₇   F
Down came the rain and   washed the spi-der out.
See the little   puffer-billies   all   in a   row.

F   F   C₇   F
Out   came the sun and   dried up all the rain, And the
See the lit - tle   dri-ver   turn the lit-tle han- dle.

F   F   C₇   F
eency weency spi - der went up the spout a-gain.
Puff, puff!   Choo, choo!   Off   they   go!

Song: HUSH, LITTLE BABY   **First note:** D   Grades 3-6

Descant: I LOVE COFFEE   **First note:** D

G   D₇
1. Hush, little ba - by,   don't say a word,
    I   love cof-fee,   I   love tea,

D₇   G
Papa's going to buy you a   mock - ing bird.
I   love the girls and the   girls   love me.

2. If that mocking bird won't sing,
   Papa's going to buy you a diamond ring.

3. If that diamond ring turns brass,
   Papa's going to buy you a looking glass.

4. If that looking glass gets broke,
   Papa's going to buy you a billy goat.

5. If that billy goat won't pull,
   Papa's going to buy you a cart and bull.

6. If that cart and bull turn over,
   Papa's going to buy you a dog named Rover.

7. If that dog named Rover won't bark,
   Papa's going to buy you a horse and cart.

8. If that horse and cart break down,
   We'll take a walk all around the town.

Song: SHOO, FLY   **First note:** B   Grades 3-6

Descants: JIMMY CRACK CORN   **First note:** D

Chorus of POLLY WOLLY DOODLE

G G	D_7 D_7	D_7 D_7	D_7 G
Shoo, fly—, don't	both - er me,	Shoo, fly—, don't	both - er me,
Jimmy crack corn and	I don't care,	Jimmy crack corn and	I don't care,

                                                     Fine

G G	D_7 D_7	D_7 D_7	G G
Shoo, fly—, don't	both - er me, For	I be-long to	some-body.
Jimmy crack corn and	I don't care, My	mas-ter's gone a-	way.

I	G G
Fare thee	feel, I feel, I feel,
	well, fare thee well,

I	G D_7
Fare thee	feel like a morn-ing star,
	well my fair - y fay,

I	D_7 D_7
For I'm	feel, I feel, I feel ———,
	going to Louisi-ana for to see my Susy-anna

                                             D.C. al Fine

I	D^7 G
Sing	feel like a morn- ing star. So
	Polly wolly doodle all the day.

Song: HE'S GOT THE WHOLE WORLD IN HIS HANDS **First note:** C̄ Grades 3-6

Descant: THIS IS THE WAY (MULBERRY BUSH)   **First note:** F

	F	F
1. He's got the	whole world	in His hands,
(Sung slowly)	This is the way we	go to church,

	C₇	C₇
He's got the	whole world	in His hands,
	Go to church,	go to church,

	F	F
He's got the	whole world	in His hands,
	This is the way we	go to church,

	C₇	F
He's got the	whole world in His	hands.
So	ear - ly in the	morn-ing.

2. He's got the little bitty baby . . . . .

3. He's got you and me, brother . . . . .

4. He's got the wind and the rain . . . . .

Song: THE LONE STAR TRAIL   **First note:** middle C   Grades 3-6

Descant: LITTLE DAVID   **First note:** A

	F F	F F
1. I	started on the trail on	June twen -ty third.
Little David,	play on your harp, Hal-le-	lu, Hal - le - lu,

	F F	F F
I been	punchin' Texas cattle on the	Lone Star Trail,
Little David,	play on your harp, Hal - le -	lu ——

	F F	F F
Refrain: Singing	Ki - yi yippy yappy	yay, yappy yay,
Little David,	play on your harp, Hal-le-	lu, Hal -le-lu,

	F F	F F
Singing	ki - yi yippy yappy	yay —.
Little David,	play on your harp, Hal-le-	lu —.

2. It's cloudy in the west, a-lookin' like rain,
   A-and my old slicker's in the wagon again. *Refrain*

Song: FOUR IN A BOAT   **First note:** G   Grades 3-6

Descant: SHE'LL BE COMIN' 'ROUND THE MOUNTAIN   **First note:** D

	G	G	G	G
1.	Four in a	boat and the	tide rolls	high,
She'll be	comin' 'round the	mountain when she	comes——	—,

	G	G	D7	D7
	Four in a	boat and the	tide rolls	high,
She'll be	comin' 'round the	mountain when she	comes——	—,

	G	G	C
	Four in a	boat and the	tide rolls
She'll be	comin' 'round the	mountain, she'll be	comin' 'round

	C
the	high,
	mountain,

	D7	D7	G G
	Get you a	pretty one	bye and bye.
She'll be	comin' 'round the	mountain when she	comes.

2. Find you a partner and stay all day . . . . .
   We don't care what the old folks say.
3. Eight in a boat and it won't go round . . . . .
   Swing that pretty one you just found.

Song: CAMPTOWN RACES   **First note:** high C   Grades 4-6

Descant: HAIL! HAIL! THE GANG'S ALL HERE   **First note:** A

	F	F	C7
The	Camptown ladies	sing this song,	Doo - dah,
	Hail! Hail! The	gang's all here,	What the heck do we care?

	C7
	Doo - dah!
	What the heck do we care?

	F	F	
The	Camptown race track	five miles long,	
	Hail! Hail! The	gang's all here,	

C_7 | F
Oh,   doo - dah | day!
What the heck do we   care | now?

| F | F | C_7
I | come down there with my | hat   caved in, | Doo - dah,
  | Hail!   Hail!   the | gang's all   here, | What the heck do we care? |

C_7
Doo - dah!
What the heck do we care?

| F | F
I | go back home with a | pocket full of tin,
  | Hail! Hail!   the | gang's all   here, |

C_7 | F
Oh,   doo-dah | day!
What the heck do we   care | now? |

                    F | F B^b | F
Song alone: Going to run all | night, Going to run all | day.

                                      | F | F
Song and descant: I'll | bet my money on the | bob - tail nag,
                              | Hail!   Hail!   the | gang's all here, |

C_7 | F
Some - body   bet on the | bay.
What the heck do we care | now? |

Song: GOOD-NIGHT, LADIES   **First note:** F   Grades 4-6

Descants: WHEN THE SAINTS GO MARCHING IN   **First note:** F

          THE OLD GRAY MARE   **First note:** high C

                  | F | F | F | C_7
                  | Good night, | ladies! | Good   night, | ladies
O, when the | saint s go marching | in, O, when the | saints go marching | in—

                  | F | B^b | C_7 | F
                  | Good   night, | ladies! We're | going to leave you | now.
O then I | want to be in that | number When the | saints go marching | in.

F	F
Mer - ri - ly we	roll a - long,

O, the | old gray mare, she | ain't what she used to be,

C₇	F
Roll a - long,	roll a - long,
Ain't what she used to be,	ain't what she used to be.

F	F	C₇ F
Mer - ri - ly we	roll a - long	O'er the bright blue sea.

The | old gray mare, she | ain't what she used to be | Many long years   a - go.

HARMONIZING WITH AN OSTINATO

An ostinato is a short phrase of music that has been composed so as to sound well when it is repeated at intervals with a piece of music. Any phrase of a round could be used as an ostinato with the round. For example, while the round "Are You Sleeping?" was being sung, the last phrase, "Ding, ding, dong," could be sung as an ostinato throughout.

Not all songs are suited for ostinato accompaniment. The best would be those with few chord changes in the harmony and that have a definite rhythm. The chief value of the ostinato as a means of accompanying a song is that it is very easy to do. Just about anyone can repeat a short phrase against another background.

There is a drawback to using an ostinato; in time, the sound tends to seem monotonous and boring. There is a possibility that both singers and listeners may become partially mesmerized or experience various unpleasant physical sensations, like people driving on straight, unbroken concrete highways with no variation in scenery. Eventually, they might have feelings of slight nausea, irritability, sleepiness, dizziness, etc. Never ask a group of children to repeat an ostinato continuously for any length of time.

To prevent bad effects from repetition of an ostinato, try varying it. Have it sung at different volumes—loudly one time, close to a whisper at another. It can be sung with the words and syllables cut short one time, drawn out another. It can be sung on a neutral syllable like "loo," or it can be hummed rather than sung with words.

An ostinato can be sung by either half or a third of the whole group of singers. Teach the ostinato to everyone; make sure everyone knows the song well. It is important that both parts keep a strict rhythm. If necessary, have everyone clap the steady beat of the song while singing.

If the music of the ostinato gives the learners any problems, you could start by having everyone speak the syllable note names in the rhythm of the notes. When they are able to do that well, have the notes sung. Finally, have it sung with words.

The ostinato can be used as an introduction to the song it is to accompany. This means that the singers of the song need to know their starting note in relation to the last note of the ostinato. The ostinato will be sung once or twice. The next time it is sung, the song will be started. It is a good idea to give the melody singers their starting pitch and have them hum it for a few seconds so that they will remember it. Then give the ostinato singers their pitch and have them start. You or a child leader will then give a hand signal to bring in the singers of the song.

Songs with Ostinato

LITTLE RED CABOOSE (Traditional American Song)   Grades 1-4

Ostinato
so so so so so la   so so so so so la..
Chug-a chug-a chug-a   Chug-a chug-a chug-a....

Song: First note—G (so)

C   C   C   C
Little red caboose, - - - little red caboose, - - -

C   C   G₇   G₇
Little red caboose behind the train, the train,

G₇   G₇ G₇   G₇
Smokestack on its back, comin' down the track,

G₇   G₇   C   C
Little red caboose behind the train, the train.

TRAIN IS A-COMING (Spiritual)   Grades 2-4

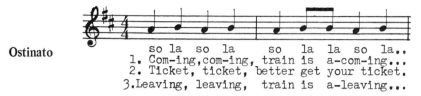

Ostinato

so la so la   so la la so la..
1. Com-ing, com-ing, train is a-com-ing...
2. Ticket, ticket, better get your ticket.
3. Leaving, leaving, train is a-leaving...

Song: First note–D (do)

    D   D   D   D
1. Train is a-coming, oh, yes,

    D   D A_7 A_7
Train is a-coming, oh, yes,

    D   D   D   D
Train is a-coming, train is a-coming,

    D   D   D   D
Train is a-coming, oh, yes.

2. Better get your ticket . . . . .
3. Train is a-leaving . . . . .

OLD MACDONALD HAD A FARM (Traditional)   Grades 2-4

Ostinato

do do do so la la so   la la so la la so
Old MacDonald had a farm, had a farm, had a farm..

(Note: As the song progresses other words may be substituted in the ostinato which will correspond to the words of the text.)

Song: First note–G (do)

   G   G   C   G   G D_7 G G
1. Old MacDonald had a farm, E - - I - - E - - I - - O!

     G   G   C   G   G D_7 G G
And on this farm he had some chicks, E - - I - - E -I - - O!

     G   G   G   G
With a chick, chick here, and a chick, chick there,

  G   C   G   C
Here a chick, there a chick, ev'rywhere a chick, chick,

G	G	C	G	G	D$_7$	G	G

Old MacDonald had a farm, E - - I - - E - - I - - O!

2. . . . . .some ducks . . . . . (quack, quack)

3. . . . . . some turkeys . . . . . (gobble, gobble)

4. . . . . . some pigs . . . . . (oink, oink)

5. . . . . . a truck . . . . . (rattle, rattle)

WHEN JOHNNY COMES MARCHING HOME (Louis Lambert)   Grades 2-6

Ostinato

Song: First note—G (la)

g min.   g min.   B^b B^b

1. When Johnny comes marching home again, Hurrah! Hurrah!

g min.   g min.   B^b D$_7$

We'll give him a hearty welcome then, Hurrah! Hurrah!

B^b D^7

The men will cheer, the boys will shout,

g min.   D$_7$

The ladies they will all turn out,

B^b D$_7$ g min. D$_7$ g min.   g min.

And we'll all feel gay   when Johnny comes marching home!

2. Get ready for the jubilee, Hurrah! Hurrah!
   We'll give the hero three times three, Hurrah! Hurrah!
   The laurel wreath is ready now
   To place upon his loyal brow,
   And we'll all feel gay when Johnny comes marching home!

SHE'LL BE COMIN' 'ROUND THE MOUNTAIN (Traditional)   Grades 3-6

Ostinato: The note pattern is the same except for the end of the third phrase. The children should hear the change in the harmony when the ostinato is sung with the song and automatically use the correct notes.

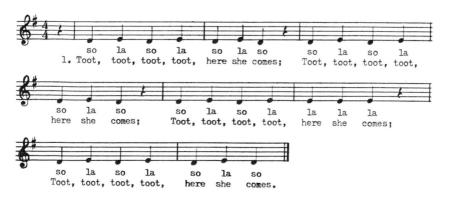

2. Whoa, back, whoa, back, here she comes . . . . .
3. Hi, Babe! Hi, Babe! here she comes . . . . .
4. Chop, chop, chop, chop, here she comes . . . . . .
5. Yum, yum, yum, yum, here she comes . . . . .

Song: First note—low D (so)

       G   G
1. She'll be comin' 'round the mountain when she comes,

       G D_7
She'll be comin' 'round the mountain when she comes,

       G   C
She'll be comin' 'round the mountain, she'll be comin'
                   'round the mountain,

      D_7 G
She'll be comin' 'round the mountain when she comes.

2. She'll be drivin' six white horses . . . . .
3. We will all go down to meet her . . . . .
4. We will kill the old red rooster . . . . .
5. We will all have chicken 'n' dumplings . . . . .

POLLY WOLLY DOODLE (American Folk Song)   Grades 3-6

Song: First note–F (do)

              F   F
1. Oh, I went down South to see my Sal,

              F   C₇
Sing Polly wolly doodle all the day;

        C₇   C₇
My Sally is a spunky gal

        C₇   F
Sing Polly wolly doodle all the day.

                    F   F
Refrain: Fare thee well, fare thee well,

              F   C₇
Fare thee well my fairy fay,

            C₇   C₇
For I'm going to Louisiana, for to see my Susyanna,

        C₇   F
Sing Polly wolly doodle all the day.

2. My Sally is a maiden fair, Sing . . . . .
   With curly eyes and laughing hair, Sing . . . . . *Refrain*
3. Behind the barn, down on my knees, Sing . . . . .
   I thought I heard a chicken sneeze, Sing . . . . . *Refrain*
4. He sneezed so hard with whoopin' cough, Sing . . . . .
   He sneezed his head and tail right off, Sing . . . . . *Refrain*

OH, SUSANNA (S. Foster)   Grades 3-6

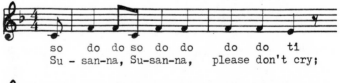

Song:First note—F (do)

     F   F   F   C₇
1. I came from Alabama with my banjo on my knee,

       F   F   F   C₇   F
I'm going to Louisiana, my true love for to see.

    F   F   F   C₇
It rained all night the day I left, the weather it was dry,

     F   F   F C₇   F
The sun so hot I froze to death; Susanna, don't you cry.

     B♭   B♭   F   C₇
Refrain: Oh, Susanna! Oh, don't you cry for me,

   F   F   F C₇   F
I've come from Alabama with my banjo on my knee.

2. I had a dream the other night, when ev'rything was still;
   I thought I saw Susanna, a-coming down the hill;
   The buckwheat cake was in her mouth, the tear was in her eye;
   Says I, I'm coming from the South, Susanna, don't you cry.

Refrain

THE MORE WE GET TOGETHER (German Folk Song)   Grades 4-6)

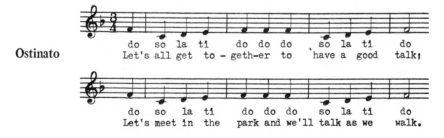

Ostinato

do so la ti   do do do   so la ti   do
Let's all get to - geth-er to have a good talk;

do so la ti   do do do so la ti   do
Let's meet in the park and we'll talk as we walk.

Song: First note—F (do)

      F   F   C₇   F
The more we get together, together, together,

F   F   C₇   F

   F   F   C$_7$ F

The more we get together, the happier we'll be.

C$_7$ F   C$_7$ F

For your friends are my friends, and my friends are your friends,

   F   F   C$_7$ F

The more we get together, the happier we'll be.

THERE'S MUSIC IN THE AIR (G. F. Root)   Grades 4-6

Ostinato

so   do do do   so   do do do so
There's mu-sic ring-ing, sweet-ly sing - ing,

ti ti ti so   do do do
Ring - ing, sing-ing in the air.

Song: First note–D (so)

      G   C-G D$_7$ G

1. There's music in the air When the infant morn is nigh,

      G   C–G D$_7$ G

And faint its blush is seen On the bright and laughing sky.

C   G   D$_7$ G

Many a harp's ecstatic sound Thrills us with a joy profound,

C   G   D$_7$ G

While we list enchanted there To the music in the air.

2. There's music in the air When the twilight's gentle sigh
   Is lost on ev'ning's breast, As its pensive beauties die.
   Then, oh, then the loved ones gone Wake the pure celestial song,
   Angel voices greet us there In the music in the air.

HARMONIZING WITH NOTES OF CHORDS

A chord in music is a combination of three or more harmonious tones. Every melody is accompanied by a succession of chords which are either heard faintly as overtones or which are sounded by an accompaniment. Because every note of melody has its own chord implied, a chordal accompaniment must be based on the dictates of overtones. The composer or accompanist is limited by the melody to a large extent. However, since there are always three or more notes in every chord, he is free to choose the ones he wants to feature.

The musical arranger chooses single notes from the chords accompanying every melody note and tries to make an interesting and pleasing sequence. For instance, he might have them progress back and forth from a higher note to a lower—up, down, up, down—as when a tuba goes "oom-pa, oom-pa." Or he might have them "shadow" the notes of the melody, keeping a certain interval away. If possible, a single-note harmony might wander up and down the scale.

In the songs that follow, the notes selected for harmonizing the melodies are close to each other. This will make it easy for you and your children to sing them. The letter names of chords that can be played on a chording instrument appear over the words; the use of an accompaniment is optional and should be used only after the singers have learned to sing the harmony independently.

If necessary, prepare the children for this activity by having them review the scale thoroughly (pages 37-40). Write the scale names on the board in ascending and descending order and have the scale sung up and down on syllables. Then have the singers practice singing intervals. Use a pointer and move it back and forth on some of the notes that may be needed. The intervals they will need to know will be those of a second, a third, and a fourth. For example, you might drill them as follows, always starting on "do." Point back and forth to do, re, do, re, do, re, mi, do, mi, do, mi, fa, so, so, so, do, so, do, so, etc.

The words of the song should be written on the chalk board, and the note names of the harmony part should appear over the appropriate words or syllables. If necessary, teach the song by rote. Give the pitch of the first note of the harmony part, and point to each note name in turn while it is sung.

When both the song and the harmony are known by all singers, divide them into two sections. Have each section sing its part alone, and check it for balance. Be sure the harmony singers know that they sing note names, not words. If they learn the notes well enough, they may eventually sing them on a neutral syllable like "loo."

To put song and harmony together, give the pitch of the first note to the harmony singers. While they hum it lightly, give the melody singers their pitch. (If the pitch is the same, this is not necessary.) Singers should hum the two pitches until the tones blend. Signal the humming to stop by dropping your hand. When you raise it, the singing should begin.

Songs Accompanied by Notes of Chords

AULD LANG SYNE (Scotch tune)   Grades 3-6

First note: middle C (so)   **Harmony notes**: do, ti in half notes

```
          F                 C7
          do (F)– do ——— ti ——— ti ——
      Should auld   acquaintance be   for - got
      For    auld     lang     syne, my  dear,
```

```
          F                 Bb
          do —— do ——— do — do——
      And nev - er  brought to mind?
      For auld     lang       syne;
```

```
          F                 C7
          do ——do ——— ti ——— ti ——
      Should auld acquaintance be    for - got
      We'll   take a cup  o'    kind-ness yet
```

```
          F      C7      F
          do —— ti ——— do — do ——
      And days of  auld lang syne?
      For auld     lang     syne.
```

YANKEE DOODLE (Traditional)   Grades 4-6

First note: G (do)   **Harmony notes**: mi, fa, so, la in quarter notes

```
      G      G      G      D7     G      G  G  D7
      mi (B)–so —— mi —— so —— mi — so— mi–so——
      Yankee Doodle came to town, Riding on a po - ny;
```

```
      G      G      C      C      D7     D7  G  G
      mi—— so —— fa — la —— so —— fa— mi–mi——
      Stuck a feather in his cap and called it Maca-ro - ni.
```

```
   C      C     C     C G    G     G   G
   fa ——fa —— fa ——fa –mi —— mi——mi—mi——
```
Chorus: Yankee Doodle keep it up, Yankee Doodle dan - dy,

```
C        C    C     C        G      D7    G   G
fa———— fa— fa——fa ———— so —— fa —— mi—mi——
```
Mind the music and the step And with the girls be han - dy.

DOWN IN THE VALLEY (American Folk Song)   Grades 4-6

First note: D (so)   **Harmonizing notes:** so, ti, do in dotted quarter notes

```
   D7          G        G      D7
   so (D) —— do—do ——do—— ti— ti——
```
1. Down in the val - ley, the valley so low,

```
   D7            D7 D7  D7          G
   so————————ti— ti— ti ————————do— do—
```
Hang your head o - ver, hear the winds blow.

2. Hear the winds blow, dear, hear the winds blow,
   Hang your head over, hear the winds blow,
3. Writing this letter, containing three lines,
   Answer my question, will you be mine?
4. Will you be mine, dear, will you be mine?
   Answer my question, will you be mine?
5. Build me a castle forty feet high,
   So I can see him as he rides by.
6. As he rides by, dear, as he rides by,
   So I can see him as he rides by.

HOME ON THE RANGE (Cowboy Song)   Grades 4-6

First note: C (so)   **Harmony notes:** so, la, ti, do in dotted quarter notes

```
   F                        Bb
   so (C) — do ———————— la    do——
```
Oh, give me a home where the buffalo roam,

```
     F                   C7
     do ———————— la ———— ti—so——
```
Where the deer and the antelope play,

F   B$\flat$
so ——— do ——— la ——— do ———
Where seldom is heard a discouraging word,

F   C$_7$ F
do ——— ti ——— do ——— do———
And the skies are not cloudy all day.

F   C$_7$ F
do —so ——— do — do ———
Chorus: Home, home on the range,

F   C$_7$
la ——— do ——ti——so———
Where the deer and the antelope play,

F   B$\flat$
so ——— do——— la ——— do———
Where seldom is heard a discouraging word,

F   C$_7$ F
do ——— ti ——— do ——do———
And the skies are not cloudy all day.

DIXIE (D.D. Emmett)   Grades 4-6

First note: G (so)   **Harmony notes:** do, re, mi, fa, so in quarter notes

C   C
do (C) —do ——— do — do ———
I wish   I was in the land of cotton,

F   F
fa——— fa ———fa —— fa ———
Old times there are not forgotten,

C   C   G$_7$ C
mi—mi ——— mi—mi ——re—re ——do——do——
Look a-way!   Look a-way!   Look a-way!   Dixie Land!

C   C
do— do——— do — do ———
In Dixie Land where I was born in,

F   F
fa —— fa —————— fa —— fa ——————
Early on one frosty mornin',

    C   C   G₇   C
    mi—mi ————————mi—mi ———————— re—re ————— do—do————
Look a-way!   Look a-way!   Look a-way!   Dixie Land!

    C   F   D   G₇
    do —— do ———— fa —fa ———— re— re —— so—so——
Then I wish I was in Dixie, Hooray!   Hooray!

    C   F   C   G₇
    do— do ——————— fa ——————— fa ————— mi ———— mi —fa ———— fa——
In Dixie Land I'll take my stand to live and die in Dixie;

    C   G₇   C   G₇ C
    mi—mi———— fa—fa—— mi ——————————— so ———————— fa————mi——
A-way,   a-way,   a-way   down   south   in   Dixie,

    C   G₇   C   G₇ C
    mi—mi—— fa—fa—— mi ——————————— so ———————— fa————mi——
A-way,   a-way,   a-way   down   south   in   Dixie.

BATTLE HYMN OF THE REPUBLIC (William Steffe)   Grades 4-6

First note: F (so)   **Harmony notes:** do, fa, so in quarter notes and rests

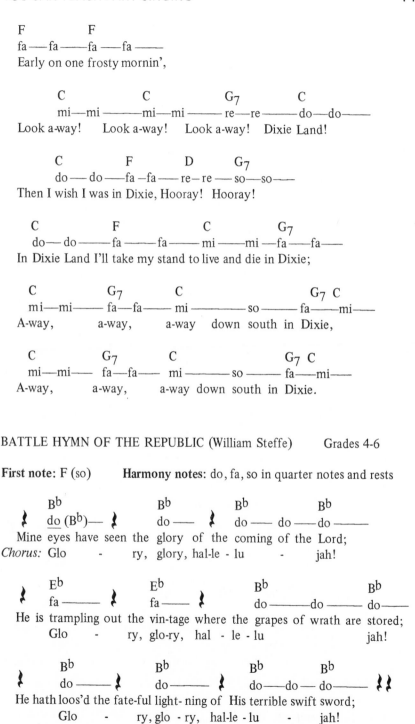

        B♭   B♭   B♭   B♭
    ⸸   do (B♭)— ⸸   do —— ⸸   do —— do —— do ————————
    Mine eyes have seen the glory of the coming of the Lord;
Chorus: Glo   -   ry, glory, hal-le - lu   -   jah!

        E♭   E♭   B♭   B♭
    ⸸   fa ———— ⸸   fa —— ⸸   do ————do ———— do——
    He is trampling out the vin-tage where the grapes of wrath are stored;
        Glo   -   ry, glo-ry, hal - le - lu   jah!

        B♭   B♭   B♭   B♭
    ⸸   do —— ⸸   do———— ⸸   do—do— do———— ⸸⸸
    He hath loos'd the fate-ful light- ning of His terrible swift sword;
        Glo   -   ry, glo - ry, hal-le - lu   -   jah!

Eᵇ   F   Bᵇ
fa —— so —— do —

His truth is marching on.
His truth is marching on.

RED RIVER VALLEY (Cowboy Song)   Grades 4-6

First note: D (so)   **Harmony notes**: mi, fa, so in half notes

        G   C
        so (D) —— mi ———————— fa ——— fa ———
1. 1. From this val-ley they say you are go - ing,
Chorus: Come and sit by my side if   you love me,

        G   D₇
        so——————— so—————so——so——
We will miss your bright eyes and sweet smile;
Do not has- ten to   bid me a - dieu;

        G   C
        so——————— mi ——————— fa———fa———
For they say you are tak- ing the sun-shine,
But re - mem-ber the Red Ri - ver Val-ley

        G   D₇   G
        so   so   mi—— mi———
That   bright-ens our path -way a - while.
And the girl   that has loved you so true.

2. Won't you think of the valley you're leaving?
   Oh, how lonely, how sad it will be!
   O-oh, think of the fond heart you're breaking,
   And the grief you are causing to me. *Chorus.*

HARMONIZING SONG ENDINGS

When a song has several chord changes, it would probably be difficult for the person untrained in music to lead a class of children to harmonize it. It would be impossible to compose an ostinato which would satisfy the chord requirements of the whole song. And it would probably be impossible to find any other song with the exact succession of chords of this song; this means that it could not be harmonized by singing it with any other.

But, it is always possible to harmonize a small part of the song which has intricate harmonic patterns. Add harmony to the last section or the last measure or two. When it is tacked on to the end only, the enrichment of sound gives the impression that this part is important, the climax of the song.

In the following songs, the harmony for the endings always starts on a note common to both melody and harmony. Have everyone in the class learn to sing the harmony using notes. Once the tune of the harmony is known, have it sung with the words of the song. Next, assign half of the singers to take the harmony part, and have them sing it alone. Then have the melody and harmony sung together, starting at the note (or notes) they have in common. Finally, everyone should sing the whole song and divide only at the part to be harmonized.

Songs with Harmonic Endings

AMERICA, THE BEAUTIFUL (Samuel Ward)   Easy

First note of song: G (so)   **Key of song:** C

Part to be harmonized: Last phrase   **First note:** G (so)

        so   la do so   fa mi
"..... From sea to shin - ing sea!"

SCHOOL DAYS (Edwards)   Easy

First note of song: B (mi)   **Key of song:** G

Part to be harmonized: Last phrase   **First note:** G (do)

        do   la la   la so so fa mi
"..... When we were a couple of kids."

OVER THE RIVER (Traditional)   Easy

First note of song: A (so)   **Key of song:** D

Part to be harmonized: Last phrase   **First note:** E (re)

        re do do do ti   ti do
"..... As o-ver the ground we go."

DECK THE HALL (Old Welsh Tune)   Medium

First note of song: C (so)   **Key of song:** F

Part to be harmonized: Last two phrases   **First note:** C (so)

```
        so    fa mi re    do  ti    do do
".....Troll the an-cient Yule-tide car-ol,

fa   fa fa fa mi  re do ti  do
Fa   la la la la   la la la la."
```

SIDEWALKS OF NEW YORK (J.W. Blake)   Medium

First note of song: high D (so)   **Key of song:** G

Part to be harmonized: Last two phrases   **First note:** G (do)

```
        do      do redo  la so so
".....Tripped the li-ight fan-tas-tic

la so so  so    fa fa   mi
On the side-walks of New York."
```

OLD FOLKS AT HOME (S. Foster)   Medium

First note of song: E (mi)   **Key of song:** C

Part to be harmonized: Last two phrases   **First note:** E (mi)

```
        mi  re  do   mi  re  do   mi   fa  fa
".....Oh, bro-thers, how my heart grows wea-ry,

mi. do   do ti  ti   ti do
Far from the old folks at home."
```

O COME, ALL YE FAITHFUL (J.F. Wade)   Medium

First note of song: G (do)   **Key of song:** G

Part to be harmonized: Refrain   **First note:** G (do)

```
        do do   ti do re do   so    do do   ti do re do   ti
".....O come, let us a - dore Him,   O come, let us a - dore Him,
```

do ti   do ti la so   la la so   fa mi mi
O come, let us a - dore Hi-im, Chri--ist, the Lord."

I'VE BEEN WORKIN' ON THE RAILROAD (American Folk Song)   Difficult

First note of song: G (do)   **Key of song:** G

Part to be harmonized: Last two sections   **First note:** B (mi)

    mi   mi   mi mi do   do do   so so
".... Some-one's in the kitch-en with Di-nah,

so   so   so so so   so so so
Some-one's in the kitch-en, I know,

so   so   so so so   so so   la la
Some-one's in the kitch-en with Di-nah,

so   so   so so fa fa   mi
Strum-min' on the old ban-jo.

so   mi mi mi   mi mi   so   so   mi mi   mi fa
Fee, Fie, Fid-dlee I O,   Fee, Fie, Fid-dlee I   O,

so   mi la la   la la so   so   so so fa fa   mi
Fee, Fie, Fid-dlee I O, Strum-min' on the old ban-jo."

STAR-SPANGLED BANNER (J.S. Smith)   Difficult

First note of song: F (so)   **Key of song:** B$^\flat$

Part to be harmonized: Last phrase   **First note:** F (so)

    so   so   mi so   do re   mi   do   la so   so fa   mi
"..... O'er the la--and of the free and the home of the brave?"

HARMONIZING WITH VOCAL CHORDINGS

Only the most capable singing groups will be able to make chords of music with their voices. This means that the activity will probably be limited to fifth- and sixth-grade children, unless there are several musically talented people in a lower class.

When a chord of music is constructed, it is usually built in the order of an original note as the lowest-sounding, the note a third above that, and the note a third above that. Call the original or root note "1" and the middle note "3," the top note "5." Do-mi-so would be in the 1-3-5 order. So would re-fa-la or so-ti-re or ti-re-fa.

But, it is not always necessary to construct a chord in the 1-3-5 order. This is because every one of these notes has corresponding notes in the octaves above and below. Think of the piano keyboard. There are eight C's, seven D's, seven E's, and so forth. If we give the same number to a note an octave away from the original note, we can construct a chord of the same notes but in a different order. For example, if we drop the 1-3 off the bottom and add it to the top, the chord will have 5 as the lowest note and 1-3. In a three-note chord, there are three possible arrangements—1-3-5, 3-5-1, and 5-1-3. To translate this into letters, a "C" chord, for instance, could be sounded C-E-G, E-G-C, or G-C-E. Or, an "F" chord could be F-A-C, A-C-F, or C-F-A.

There are advantages to being able to switch the order of notes in chords. While the harmony is always the same, the effect is different with each arrangement, something that composers and arrangers of music take advantage of all the time. Chords constructed in other than the 1-3-5 order may be helpful to singers. An inverted chord which raises or lowers notes might accommodate voices. In the song "America" (page 150), the first chord has "mi" for its lowest note. The order of this chord is 3-5-1. The third chord, however, fa-la-do, is in the 1-3-5 order.

Because the procedure for presenting lessons in making chords with voices is more complicated than the other methods of making harmony, it will be given in a step-by-step sequence. Before you start to teach a song you should make preparations on the chalk board. You must have a chart of the chords needed. Chords should be written vertically, highest notes at the top, middle and low notes under them. Over the words of the song write the chord numbers and their letter names. Have everyone sing the song. If it is not well known, it should be practiced. Then follow the steps below.

Step 1. Divide the singers into four groups and check them to make sure they are balanced in volume and in ability to hold a part. Assign one group to sing the melody and the other three groups to each take a part—high, middle or low.

Step 2. Direct attention to the chords on the board. Explain to the children that you will be giving silent signals with your fingers while the singing is going on. If they are supposed to sing chord number 1, you will hold up one finger; for chord number 2, two fingers, and so forth. Ask children in each group to name the notes they will be singing for each chord. Have a brief spoken drill with each group. Hold up one finger while they say the note name; hold up three fingers while that note is named, etc. Switch quickly.

Step 3. Have the groups practice singing their notes. You could have everyone learn to sing the notes of each part. Then have the group sing by itself.

Sound the pitch of the note of chord number 1. Hold up one finger and have the note sung. Move slowly back and forth to the other numbers. Move faster as the children become used to making changes. From time to time have frequent repeats of the same note. If the three notes of one part are re, mi, and fa, a typical drill might go: mi, fa, fa, fa, re, mi, re, mi, fa, mi, mi, mi, mi, etc. Drill the other two groups of singers in the same way.

Step 4. When they are ready, have the singers make the chords. Start with chord number 1. Give the pitch to the low group, then the middle and high groups. The three notes should be hummed lightly until they blend well. Signal with your hand to stop the humming. Then signal by holding up one finger that everyone sings the scale names of the first chord. Continue with finger signals, having the singers move very slowly at first. Drill as suggested in Step 3.

Step 5. Have the chord singers sing their chords as they will when the melody is added. If you think they need extra practice, point to the chord numbers over the song words on the board. If not, have them follow your finger signals. (You will be watching the board to know the correct order for the chords.) The chords should be sung in the rhythm of the song.

Step 6. Add the melody to the harmony. Remember that every time the song is sung, it will be necessary to have each part hum and hold its pitch until all singers are ready. You will always give finger signals to the chord singers, which means you will have to watch the numbers on the board (or on a scrap of paper or in this book) until you have memorized the sequence.

Step 7. (Optional) Have the chord singers hum their tones instead of singing them with scale names.

Step 8. (Optional) Have the chord singers sing the words of the song instead of singing notes or humming. This would be difficult for most groups because the harmony singers would have to sing in the rhythm of the melody. Do not try it unless chord singers are sure of their tones.

Songs with Vocal Chordings

AMERICA (Henry Carey)   **First note**: F (do)

Chords		
	1	2	3
High	do (F)	ti	do
Middle	so (C)	so	la
Low	mi (A)	fa	fa

1 (F)   2 (C7)
My country, 'tis of thee,

1 (F)   1 (F)
Sweet land of liberty,

2 (C7)   1 (F)
Of thee I sing;

1 (F)   1 (F)
Land where my fathers died,

2 (C7)   2 (C7)
Land of the Pilgrim's pride,

1 (F)   1 (F)
From ev'ry mountain side,

3 (Bb) 1 (F) 2 (C7) 1 (F)
Let   free - dom   ring!

FOR HE'S A JOLLY GOOD FELLOW (Traditional)   **First note**: F (do)

Chords		
	1	2	3
High	do (F)	ti	do
Middle	so (C)	so	la
Low	mi (A)	fa	fa

1 (F)   1 (F)
For he's a jolly good fellow,

2 (C7)   1 (F)
For he's a jolly good fellow,

1 (F)   3 (Bb)
For he's a jolly good fellow,

2 (C7)   1 (F)
Which nobody can de-ny.

1 (F)   3 (Bb)   1 (F)
Which nobody can   de-ny,

1 (F)   3 (Bb)   1 (F)
Which nobody can   de-ny

(Repeat first four lines)

KUM BA YAH (African Folk Song)   **First note:** D (do)

Chords			
	1	2	3
High	so (A)	la	fa
Middle	mi (F#)	fa	re
Low	do (D)	do	so

                    1 (D)   2 (G)   1 (D)
1. Kum ba yah, my Lord, Kum ba yah!

                    1 (D)   1 (D)   3 (A7)
Kum ba yah, my Lord, Kum ba yah!

                    1 (D)   2 (G)   1 (D)
Kum ba yah, my Lord, Kum ba yah!

          1 (D) 3 (A7) 1 (D)
Oh, Lord, Kum ba yah.

2. Someone's crying, Lord, Kum ba yah!
3. Someone's singing, Lord, Kum ba yah!
4. Someone's praying, Lord, Kum ba yah!

SILENT NIGHT (Franz Gruber)   **First note:** G (so)

Chords			
	1	2	3
High	so (G)	fa	la
Middle	mi (E)	re	fa
Low	do (C)	ti	do

1 (C) 1   1 (C) 1
1. Silent night! Holy night!

2 (G7) 2   1 (C) 1
All is   calm, all is bright

3 (F)   3   1 (C)   1
'Round yon virgin mother and Child,

3 (F) 3   1 (C)   1
Holy Infant so tender and mild,

2 (G7) 2   1 (C) 1
Sleep in heavenly pe-eace,

1 (C)   2 (G7) 1 (C) 1
Sleep in heavenly peace.

2. Silent night! Holy night!
Shepherds quake at the sight,
Glories stream from heaven afar,
Heav'nly hosts sing Alleluia;
Christ, the Savior, is born,
Christ, the Savior, is born.

JINGLE BELLS (J. Pierpont)   **First note**: D (so)

Chords				
	1	2	3	4
High	do (G)	do	ti	do
Middle	so (D)	la	so	la
Low	mi (B)	fa	fa	re

1 (G)   1 (G)
Dashing through the snow

1(G)   2 (C)
In a one-horse open sleigh,

2 (C)   3 (D7)
O'er the fields we go,

3 (D7)   1 (G)
Laughing all the way;

1 (G)   1 (G)
Bells on bob-tail ring,

1 (G)   2 (C)
Making spirits bright,

2 (C)   3 (D7)   3 (D7)   1 (G)
What fun it is to ride and sing / A sleighing song to-night.

1 (G)   1 (G)   1 (G)   1 (G)
Chorus: Jingle bells, jingle bells, / Jingle all the way.

2 (C)   1 (G)   4 (A)   3 (D7)
Oh, what fun it is to ride / In a one-horse open sleigh.

1 (G)   1 (G)   1 (G)   1 (G)
Jingle bells, jingle bells, / Jingle all the way.

2 (C)   1 (G)   3 (D7)   1 (G)
Oh, what fun it is to ride / In a one-horse open sleigh.

Part Three

LESSONS IN

PLAYING INSTRUMENTS

From the time they were first invented, musical instruments have been used by man to extend what he could do, to enlarge his influence on his environment. The radio is an instrument that can be played by everyone; the person who drives a car with the radio blaring is saying in effect: "Notice me. How much louder, stronger and larger am I than other people." Musicians who play electrically amplified instruments, loud drums, horns, etc., give a similar message.

When you present a pair of cymbals to one child, he may actually be afraid to play them. A more self-confident child will enjoy making them crash. The latter will probably feel comfortable with himself, willing to volunteer answers in class, etc. The former may act timid, reluctant to have people take too much notice of him. Both children think of themselves as responsible for the sounds made by the instrument they play. In the mind of a player, a musical instrument is not separate; it is a part of him.

You will find that most children are eager to play musical instruments. The strong appeal that instruments have for people is partly because their sounds are something like human sounds. A stringed instrument like the violin can sound similar to a smooth speaking voice; a woodwind instrument like the flute or clarinet can sound like a reedy-toned voice. A drum can imitate the sounds of feet stamping, hearts thumping, hands clapping, etc.

What children quickly realize is that an instrument can be made to do more and do it better than they can do with their bodies. The drum, for instance, can sound louder than stamping feet. An instrument like the flute or violin can play higher than a voice can sing; the bass instruments can go lower. The piano is a single instrument that has a far more extensive range than a single human voice. By pressing several keys the player can make it sound like several voices in harmony. The fingers of a virtuoso pianist can play the keys faster than anyone can sing. A singer must hesitate in order to breathe, but the instrumentalist can go nonstop.

Children can use instruments to make some of the sounds of the environment. Sounds of nature—thunder and lightning, things being blown by wind, a babbling brook, a crashing wave, pattering rain—can be simulated. Sounds of wild life—the twittering of a bird, the quack of a duck, the growl of an animal—can be imitated. Sounds of machines—ticking clocks, clacking typewriters, purring motors— can be made. Much popular music has a continual thumping and whirring resembling motors in its accompaniment.

People's lives are such that they cannot always have the sounds of life and living around them. But the person who plays a musical instrument can make these sounds to comfort himself any time he feels lonely or feels the need for companionship. An inhibited person can use a musical instrument to express feelings which he has repressed. An angry child can beat a drum rather than hurt himself or innocent people. The child who feels sad but cannot express it might get relief by playing a sad song on a melody instrument.

The environment contains many musical instruments. Children have only to listen and they will find them. The keys on a key ring that someone nonchalantly shakes, the glass of water which is accidentally tapped with a knife, the rubber band that twangs as it is pulled and released—such sounds will be heeded by some, ignored by others. Those who are aware and imaginative will be able to find many objects with which to make music.

You will be shown in the following chapters how to help children make and play simple instruments. In Chapter 5 the focus will be on rhythm instruments; little, if any, skill is required to play most of them. Some are played by tapping; others have parts that are banged together; still others must be shaken.

In Chapter 6 the focus will be on making melody. A melody instrument must have material which makes it possible for the player to produce different pitches. A catgut string can be stretched or loosened; when vibrated, it will make sounds of higher or lower pitch. Wood, plastic or metal tubes vibrate when air is blown into them. The tubes have holes along the length, and changes in pitch are produced by the player when he covers and uncovers the holes with the ends of his fingers, forcing the air to travel longer or shorter distances.

Because it is more difficult to make melody on an instrument than it is to make rhythm, you will only be told how to make and play simple instruments. Not only must the melody player know how to change pitch on his instrument; he must make the changes rapidly and accurately. Simultaneously, he must produce a decent tone. It can take a trumpet player years to develop the stamina needed to play for any length of time as well as to produce a pleasing tone. At the same time he must become so familiar with the fingering of notes that he is able to play them as quickly as necessary.

But making melody on an instrument need not be an overwhelming task. It takes little or no ability, for instance, to produce an acceptable tone on a xylophone, though it may take a while to learn to locate notes quickly. And everyone who can blow can make a respectable sound on a tonette or a flutophone. Only a little more skill is needed to play a recorder.

You will be shown in the following chapters how to help your children become conscious of musical instruments—what they are, how to find them, how to make them, how to play them.

Chapter 5

YOU CAN TEACH RHYTHM

WITH INSTRUMENTS

From the time they are infants, children are aware of rhythm. It is thought that mothers instinctively hold their babies so that their heads rest against the left side where heart beats can be heard. Being held in this position can calm an upset baby, probably because the rhythmical sound of her heart signifies security.

Children continue to feel reassured by rhythmical sounds. Some are human rhythms—heart beats, breathing and walking. Others are mechanical sounds that occur in rhythm—the ringing of a telephone, the ticking of a clock, the agitating of a washing machine, the stitching of a sewing machine. In fact, it seems as if people feel safer hearing the rhythmic pulsings and purrings of the various motors in and around their houses than hearing the more sporadic sounds of nature—the moving of objects by wind, people talking, etc. They try to synchronize their activities with the rhythms of the motors. Many of the people of modern cities act like dancers to unseen machines as they walk at a quick, even pace. They talk fast, as if in imitation of the tempos of the mechanized vehicles around them.

When you teach children rhythm, you take advantage of their natural inclination to enjoy and respond to rhythmical events. When you ask them to use instruments for making rhythm, you will be asking them to do something else that is done naturally. People of any age are like the first primitive person who accidentally tapped two sticks together and became aware of the pleasure the sounds gave him, probably because of their similarity to the sounds of life. The tempo at which a player will naturally move will be about the tempo of walking. Though some of his notes might move fast, there will be a regular underlying beat, organized in a pattern of strong-weak, one-two, or left-right.

The rhythm instruments which your students will use will have the possibility not only of thumping like the drums of primitive man or clicking and tapping like his sticks. Rattles like maracas or shakers will make various swishing sounds; sand blocks or jingle sticks will also swish. Another kind of sound will be produced when metal hits metal. There will be loud-crashing cymbals, chiming bells, sweetly ringing triangles, the deep ringing of gongs. Clicking sounds can be made with castanets, and grating noises can be made with scrapers.

Only certain instruments are used for making rhythm—drums, bells, rhythm sticks, maracas, etc. These are the instruments you will have in your classroom that can be used to imitate either human or mechanical rhythms. A drum, for instance, might be made to sound like a person walking in heavy boots. Or it might be made to sound like an oil pump pumping oil, a ball bouncing on a pavement, or a big machine thumping in a factory.

Sand blocks rubbed together can sound like a train putting out puffs of steam; claves or rhythm sticks can sound like the clip clop of horses' hoofs on a pavement. Triangles and finger cymbals can be played to sound like the splashing of a fountain of water into a basin or the dripping of rain on a surface.

Some of the instruments your children will use will sound faint; some will sound powerful. Therefore, you will need fewer of the latter than of the former. For instance, you should have only a few cymbals, but you will need a number of triangles. The louder instruments will be used less in ensemble playing, probably for accent only, whereas fainter instruments might be played during an entire piece of music.

When instruments are chosen or made for children, it is very important that the tone quality be interesting and pleasing. Poor tone, when coupled with lack of volume, can be annoying and discouraging for the rhythm instrument player. Homemade instruments should be made with this thought in mind. It can be frustrating for a child to tap a small oatmeal box with a pencil if he hears neither a good tone nor much sound. On the other hand, tapping a heavy pie tin that is being held by a handle, and which gives off a clear and resonant tone, can be a satisfying experience. A jar full of dried beans can make a pleasant swishing sound.

When your children play their rhythm instruments, they will use only certain rhythms and tempos. Most used will be the rhythm which goes at the rate of speed of walking. Even a melody which has a combination of speeds will have a steady beat, beat, beat, beat underlying it. Those rhythms which naturally group in three's or six's are usually performed at a fast rate which causes them to fall into the walk pattern—one-two, step-step, left-right.

Another popular rhythm will be an eighth-note rhythm which goes as fast as a slow run. For many children this is difficult to control, either when done with the feet or with the hands. The tendency, especially with young children, is to assume that all that is required is that they move very quickly. You may need to guide them to restrain them from going too fast. If you are uncertain about how fast to go, find a familiar song like "Yankee Doodle" which has several eighth notes and learn from it how to express this rhythm.

Another rhythmic requirement of the player of instruments is that he be able to play a single beat and rest for the remainder of a measure. Those who play the instruments used for emphasis—drums, gongs, cymbals, etc.—will often play this way.

A rhythm that is easy to play is the rhythm of skipping: People use this rhythm when they feel joy or exuberance. A hesitation step on one foot is followed by a quick hop to the other. If the children have difficulty playing this rhythm, suggest that they picture themselves skipping or that they do a few skips with their feet and transfer what they have done to their hands.

Rhythm instruments can usually be played by almost anyone without practice. What might give some children a problem is keeping a rhythm. But the motions which must be made are done with hands and arms. Early man and his predecessors used their arms for climbing trees as well as for carrying things, bringing food to the mouth, etc. We have inherited bodies that are essentially the same. We have hands with opposing thumbs which can grasp objects. It is natural for us to swing our arms away from each other and to bring them together. One of the first activities adults encourage in a baby is to play "pat-a-cake." People clap hands as a sign of approval and an expression of joy. When objects are held in each hand, it is easy for the person to bring them together.

The other motions needed for playing rhythm instruments are also natural and easy to make. Shaking an object held in the hand and beating down on a drum are the same motion and are easy to do. Sliding the hands back and forth past each other, the motion used for playing sand blocks, and opening and closing the hand to play castanets are not difficult movements.

BECOMING AWARE OF SOUND

In our immediate environment there is much sound that we realize is there but which we mentally "tune out." If we were to pay attention to every sound that we heard during a day, it could be tiring and perhaps nerve-racking; it could prevent us from thinking about anything else. However, because in the lessons that follow you will be asking your children to work with sound—making their own instruments, discovering instruments, choosing instruments for accompaniment, deciding on "orchestrations," etc.—it is important to help them notice sounds in the environment.

Lessons in Noticing Sound

Tell the children that you would like everyone to be silent for a period of time (one to two minutes, depending on their age and attention span). They should listen to the sounds around them. Most children need to close their eyes while they listen.

When time is up, ask the children to tell you what they heard. They will name such things as the hum of fluorescent lights, the clock ticking, radiators popping, people in other areas of the building talking and moving, things being blown by wind, people breathing, someone's stomach rumbling, vehicles passing on the street outside, insects buzzing, birds singing, and so on.

Next, ask everyone what information was communicated by the sounds. They may have learned about the weather, about what was going on out of doors, about what was happening in the rest of the building, etc. Ask them to tell which sounds were made by people. Which were made by animals, by birds, by other creatures? Which were made by motors or mechanical devices?

How did the children feel about the sounds? Were they frightened by any? Did they enjoy any? Did any sounds make them laugh? Were they annoyed by any of them?

Ask for descriptions of the sounds. Which seemed loudest? Which would have been loudest if they had been next to it or them? Which sounds were the most difficult to hear? Which sound was farthest away? Which was nearest? Did any sound become louder or softer while it was being made? Which was the highest pitch? Which was lowest? Were any sounds done in rhythm?

Did anyone think that any of the sounds were musical? To be musical, a sound need not be made by a musical instrument, a singing voice or by groups of instruments or voices. To some people, the sounds of a broom sweeping seem musical. To others, the sounds of an empty trash can bouncing are pleasing, though most people would call them noise.

Such a lesson can be brief; it can be repeated in a variety of ways. For instance, the children can be taken on a walk out-of-doors, or they can be taken on a walk through the school, or they might sit in the school cafeteria or the auditorium and listen to the sounds around them. If there is a chance they will forget what they have heard, have everyone carry a notebook and pencil with which to take notes. The children's findings can be discussed when you get back to the classroom.

DISCOVERING RHYTHM INSTRUMENTS

It is by chance observation that people make discoveries and inventions. Each musical instrument has been discovered by some person who happened to notice the sounds made by objects in his environment. In most cases the objects became instruments only after they were modified, re-shaped to improve the tone, etc.

Among the most recently invented instruments are the "pans" of the West Indies. Someone noticed that a fifty-gallon steel oil drum made a ringing tone when it was hit and that the pitch changed when it was hit in different places. To make an instrument, the ends of the drums are trimmed down with a hacksaw or blow torch to the desired size. Then indentations are made around the head with a heavy hammer. These produce tones of different pitches when hit with mallets. In ensemble, the pans are called "steel bands."

Some people are more aware of sound than are others. There are several stories about the sensitivity of great composers as children. The musically-gifted child would be observed listening attentively to the sounds of water boiling, a tea kettle whistling, a shutter banging in the wind, birds calling, a floor board squeaking, a door creaking, rain tapping on a surface, etc. Your children need this kind of awareness if they are to make discoveries.

It is not uncommon for teachers of art to encourage students to take materials from their environment and remake them to create an aesthetic effect. The person who can recognize beauty in a sea shell or a piece of driftwood has developed visual awareness. Students of music can be trained to have aural sensitivity.

Lessons in Discovering Rhythm Instruments

Begin a lesson by asking your children to look around them and imagine what objects could make sounds in rhythm. If they seem to need stimulation, leave a few items—a bunch of keys on a key ring, pencils and rulers, boxes of paper clips or thumb tacks—in plain sight. Without saying anything, give them ideas. You could walk across the floor by shuffling your feet, making a rhythmical swishing sound as you move. Click the mechanism of a ballpoint pen. Open the door of the room a few inches; then close and open it in rhythm. Once they have the idea, the children will make a lot of original discoveries.

Assign everyone to look around home for objects to bring to school to play as rhythm instruments. They should test the items they consider and bring in only those with pleasing sound. They should not buy materials, nor should they make anything. Suggest that they look in the kitchen, the play room, the home woodworking shop, tool boxes, back yards, etc.

Objects such as the following are suitable: boxes of nails, pins, hair pins, rice, macaroni, grains, etc.; empty jars, cans and boxes and something with which to hit them; the reflector pan from under a stove burner; hub caps, brake drums, and other parts of cars; parts from discarded washing machines or other machinery; piggy banks with money; forks and spoons, curtain rods, pots and pans, clay pots, stones and rocks. Discourage the children from bringing in potentially dangerous items. A light bulb, for instance, will shatter when dropped; a sharp knife could cut someone.

Suggest that the children play their "instruments" in turn, and have them notice the differences in tone in similar objects. Compare the sound from a box of pins being shaken with that of a box of nails. They can experiment by tapping the same object with a nail, with a pencil, and with a ruler. Ask them to play their "instruments" in different ways—perhaps loud and soft, fast and slow. Give them time to get familiar with them.

There are various ways to put rhythm makers to use. First, group the "instruments" by categories. If a child has brought in more than one, he should choose the one he wants for each exercise. The groups should be assigned areas. For example, children with rhythm makers that are played by shaking would get together; those with "instruments" that are played by metal hitting metal would be in another section; those having wood hitting wood would assemble, etc. You would have as many categories as needed.

Try some question-and-answer improvisation. You will need three groups. One would be the "beat" players who keep the pulse; the second would ask the question, and the third would answer. (See a discussion of the presentation of question-and-answer phrase concepts starting on page 24 of Chapter 1.) Instead of speaking and singing questions and answers to each other, the children will be speaking and playing them on their "instruments."

Choose a group leader from the question group and one from the answer group. Each leader should write a short, easy question about general information on a piece of paper. When everyone is ready, those who play the beat start playing at a steady walk rhythm, keeping their playing soft enough so that the voice of the person asking the question or giving the answer can be heard. Next, Child 1, the leader of Group 1, asks the first question, speaking so that his voice fits with the steady beats. His group, Group 1, plays the question on their rhythm makers, imitating his rhythm. Without hesitating, the leader of Group 2, Child 2, must speak the answer, making his voice fit with the steady beats of the "beat" players. The rhythm of the answer is immediately played by Group 2 on their "instruments." Child 2, the leader of Group 2, speaks his question; his group plays the rhythm of the words. Child 1 speaks the answer, and Group 1 plays the rhythm.

The following is an example of question-and-answer improvisation. The group that plays the steady beat starts and continues to play throughout the exercise.

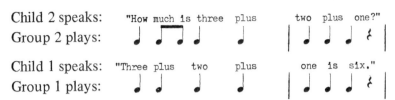

Child 2 speaks: "How much is three plus two plus one?"
Group 2 plays:

Child 1 speaks: "Three plus two plus one is six."
Group 1 plays:

The exercise can be done on other days so that every group has its share of turns at keeping the pulse and so that every child has at least one turn at being a leader.

In another exercise the children can use their "instruments" to play the rhythm of the words of a familiar song. For this there should be two groups, one to play the "question" phrases, the other the "answers."

A good procedure is to have the children sing the song through to refresh everyone's memory of the words and their rhythm. Then, have it sung again while the rhythm of the words is clapped. Next, assign the groups to take turns by phrases. The "question" group will start. They should sing and clap the first phrase while the others listen. Without hesitation, the "answer" group should sing and clap the second phrase. The first group then sings and claps the third phrase which has a questioning tone, and the second group responds. The groups continue thus to the end of the song.

Finally, tell the children to think the song and play the rhythm of the words phrase by phrase on their "instruments." Older or more capable children may be able to do this exercise with fewer steps. Younger children may need to rehearse some of the steps a number of times.

Almost any song the children know will work well with this procedure. Have them try songs that have solo voice and chorus, songs like "Swing Low, Sweet Chariot," "Li'l 'Liza Jane," and "Alouette." Have them use a group playing softer instruments on the solo parts and a group making heavier sound on the choruses.

GETTING AND MAKING RHYTHM INSTRUMENTS

In recent years, school children have been expected to use only certain instruments for making rhythm. Their music textbooks suggest that songs be accompanied by these instruments, and catalogs offer them for purchase. Among those most commonly suggested are tambourines, rhythm sticks, cymbals, triangles, bells, maracas, sand blocks, tone blocks, and various kinds of drums. If you were to equip your classroom with rhythm instruments, you would be buying these and a few other instruments.

However, it is not necessary to buy all of your instruments. Many of them can be made by you and the children. One of the big advantages to making them is that money would be saved. In many cases it is possible to produce instruments with as good quality as the purchased counterparts. The tone of rhythm sticks, for instance, is exactly the same, whether you make them of inexpensive pieces of dowel and finish them yourself or buy them ready-made and painted. Not all instruments can be duplicated easily, and you might want to buy such items as finger cymbals, tambourines, tone or wood blocks with hollowed-out bodies, and well-made drums.

Another reason for having the children make their own instruments is to give them a chance to find out how various sounds are produced and to study the components of sound—tone quality, volume, resonance, pitch, clarity, etc.

A third reason for making instruments is that it can be done easily. Any project that is successful is enjoyable. The children will automatically appreciate what they have made and will tend to give it better care than what has been bought for them.

Materials for making instruments are readily available. Some, like burnt-out light bulbs, baby food jars, grains of rice, bottle caps, etc., can be brought from home. Others can be bought at small cost from lumber companies, hardware and second-hand stores.

Storage of Rhythm Instruments

Having a "place for everything and everything in its place" is very important. If all instruments are thrown together in one box, there is a good chance that some will be damaged. But most important, it can be difficult to locate what you need if everything is in a jumble. You should have a minimum of four compartments in which to keep the collection of instruments.

If you wish to keep costs down, use cardboard boxes. These are free at the grocery store. They are durable and lightweight. They can be painted, each in a different color, for quick identification. They may be left separate, or they can be joined together, using short bolts with nuts and washers.

If you decide to join the boxes, you will in effect be making them into a single large box with sections. Try to get four or six small, but deep, boxes of the same size. A good size would be 8″ by 11″ and at least 10″ deep. Place the boxes together in the arrangement you want, and fasten the sides with four 3/8-inch bolts and nuts with washers to keep the cardboard from tearing. You can have two washers for each bolt and nut if you use the tops and bottoms of small frozen-fruit-juice cans. Drill holes in the centers large enough to push the bolts through.

You can make a base without adding much weight to the container by attaching pieces of 1″ by 2″ wood cut to length. Put one on each side along the bottom using flat-headed bolts with washers and nuts. Get bolts long enough to go through the one-inch wood and the cardboard.

Organize the storage container to suit your needs. One section might hold sticks, sand blocks and claves; a second might be for triangles, bells and jingle sticks; the third could have maracas, shakers and tambourines; and the fourth could be for castanets, cymbals and finger cymbals. Sketches or pictures of the instruments on the sides of the sections could indicate where each is supposed to be stored.

The Instruments

The paragraphs below, which describe each of the instruments, will give you the following information:

- A description of the instrument (if it might be unfamiliar)
- Directions for making the instrument (unless this is not possible or practicable)
- How to play it and how to hold it at rest
- Some of the principal ways the instrument is used
- How many instruments needed for a class of twenty-five to thirty children. (This number will depend on the loudness of an instrument. For instance, because the strength of a single pair of rhythm sticks is much less than the strength of a pair of cymbals, a rhythm instrument collection should contain a larger number of sticks than cymbals. It also happens that rhythm sticks have a tone that is more useful than the explosive crash of cymbals, and for this reason there should be more of them.)

Bells. Small bells from a horse's harness or any bells of about a half-inch diameter, the type that are used to decorate gifts, Christmas trees, wreaths, etc., can become rhythm instruments. If a bell can be attached to a wooden handle, it can be played singly. If bells are small, use several for a single instrument.

To make a single-bell instrument, use a bell of about three-quarter-inch diameter. Pass a nail through the fastener part of the bell and hammer it into the end of a piece of half-inch dowel six inches long.

If the bells are small, put a series of three to six on a stick about the size of a ruler. Space them about an inch apart along one end of the stick, leaving the other end for a handle. Nail them with small nails, and bend the points of the nails over on the back with a pair of pliers. Cover the back with a strip of decorators' adhesive tape.

Small bells can be attached to an elasticized band to be worn on the wrist or ankle. Use elastic three-quarters of an inch wide. Cut pieces to fit children's wrists or ankles, and sew the ends together. Sew three to five small bells spaced equally. Use heavy thread.

The open-ended bell with attached tongue is usually tuned to a definite pitch and is not usually used in the rhythm ensemble. Such a bell is larger and louder than the enclosed bell with a ball of metal left loose inside. If you include any in your collection, they may be used for accent.

To play the small bell or bells on a stick the player holds the stick in one hand and shakes it. The bells on the elasticized band can be worn on the wrist or held in the hand and shaken. When they are worn on the ankles, they will shake when the person moves or dances. The open-ended bell must be held by the handle at the top so the fingers do not touch the bell. After any bell has been shaken or when it is not being played, it can be damped by the player's free hand. It should be held by the hand which shakes it; the other hand should hold the metal until time to play.

You will find uses for bells during the singing of songs about sleighs or horses wearing bells, about door bells, telephones, the carts of ice cream vendors, etc. Bells can be worn on ankles when singing and dancing certain American Indian songs, gypsy songs, etc.

> Have 8 single bells on a stick, 4 minimum.
> Have 4 sets of bells on a board, 1 minimum.
> Have 12 sets of bells on elastic bands, 4 minimum.
> Have 4 open-ended bells, 1 minimum.

Castanets. The name "castanet" is derived from the Latin word for chestnut. Castanets are always in pairs. They are made from hard wood which has been hollowed out and shaped like halves of chestnuts, connected at the top by cords. This is the instrument of Spanish dancers. Castanets are held in the hand and clapped together to make clicking sounds.

If you purchase castanets that can be manipulated by children, they will probably be hinged and attached to the end of a stick. To play real castanets takes a special technique which it would take a while to learn.

You can make a small instrument that can be played with one hand, somewhat like playing real castanets. For each instrument you will need two metal bottle caps, some sturdy cardboard, heavy yarn and glue. Lay the bottle caps on a hard surface and flatten them with a hammer. Cut a strip of cardboard one and one-half inches wide by four inches long. Glue a cap to each end of the cardboard. Fold the cardboard in half so that the caps come together. The fold will act as a hinge. If it is weak, reinforce it with decorators' or electricians' tape. Use a large needle to attach a loop of yarn to each end directly over each bottle cap and on the outside. One loop will go around the player's thumb; the other will go around his first two fingers.

Clappers that will make clicking sounds something like the sounds of castanets can be made from two pieces of wood tied to a roller. The roller can be a small-sized spool, the kind on which thread is wound. For wood use two six-inch lengths of one- by two-inch lumber. Drill small holes that will be large enough to pull strong string or twine through. There should be two holes side by side going through the side of the spool and through both pieces of wood at the center. Put the spool between the two pieces of wood. Thread a large needle with heavy string or twine, and bring it down through the top piece of wood, into the spool, into the bottom piece of wood, and up through the other holes. Tie it snugly on top.

Bottle-cap castanets are held in one hand by the thumb and first two fingers. They are played by closing the hand. Because the sound is light, players can play two, one in each hand. During periods of rest, caution the players to keep their hands still.

The player of "clapper" castanets holds the instrument between both hands. The hands should be flattened in "praying" position. They are rocked back and forth, making a quick rubbing motion so that first one end of the pieces of wood is rapped, then the other end. Players should hold their instruments still during rest periods.

Spanish and Mexican dancers click castanets while dancing, and clappers are used in some Chinese dances. These instruments can be played to imitate the snapping of a turtle, to sound like train wheels clicking along a track, a mill wheel clicking as it goes around, etc.

Have 20 bottle-cap castanets, 8 minimum.

Have 8 "clapper" castanets, 2 minimum.

Claves. A claves is a pair of heavy sticks. They are played like rhythm sticks, but, because they are larger in diameter, the tone they produce is lower pitched.

To make a claves, use a piece of one-inch dowel or an old broom handle. Cut two nine-inch lengths for each instrument.

To play the claves, the player holds one stick and hits it with the other. When not playing, he can rest the ends of the sticks against his shoulders.

Claves can sound like horses' hoofs on a pavement, like a carpenter hammering, a wood cutter chopping wood, etc. They can be used to accompany songs about the dances of such places as Italy, Israel, Mexico, the West Indies, etc.

Have 10 claves (pairs of sticks), 2 minimum.

Cymbals. The brass cymbals of an orchestra or a band produce a clear, ringing tone. This can be simulated by a pair of metal pot lids or metal pie tins. Pot lids must be of the same size and can have no ridges around the rim. If there is a choice of pie tins, you can find those with the best tone by testing them. Do not hold them in the hand, as the hand damps out vibrations. Make a sling out of string, suspend the tin, and hit it with a drum mallet.

Attach a handle in the center of each pie tin chosen. Use a small cabinet door handle, or make a strap out of heavy cloth tape about an inch wide. About eighteen inches of tape will be needed for each handle. Fold the tape in half and knot the loose ends together. Drill a hole an eighth-inch in diameter in the center of each pie tin. Insert a large-sized crochet hook in the hole and pull the tape through by its fold.

Cymbals cannot be sounded if they are held in the hand, and some children need to be shown how to hold them by their handles. While waiting to play, the player should hold them in his hands in front of himself and about six inches apart. To play, the hands can be swept past each other, one hand moving up while the other moves down, both coming together as they pass. Another way to play cymbals is to hit them together quickly, as if bouncing them off each other.

No parade or march music would sound right without an occasional crash of cymbals. This instrument is used mostly for accents and to create a sense of urgency. Cymbals are sometimes used in songs about China, songs about the market places in countries around the Mediterranean, etc. They can be used to make loud sounds like the crack of thunder, the banging of garbage collectors, the pickaxing of miners and the crashing sounds made by various other workers.

If cymbals are small—four to six inches in diameter—have 6 pairs, 3 minimum. If they are large, there can be fewer.

Drums. A drum is a hollow cylinder which can be made of wood or metal. One or both ends can be covered. The material of the covering must be kept stretched tight, and it must produce a resonant sound when it is beat by the hand or a stick.

It is difficult to make a really well-toned drum. If you can afford it, buy one or more good drums with at least a twelve-inch diameter.

If you decide to make a drum, it should be easy for you to find a cylinder. Look for something that is at least six inches in diameter. A pail, a large can or canister, and a waste-paper basket are among possible metal frames. A small wooden keg, a round hat box and a round wooden container for a flower pot are some of the wood or cardboard possibilities. If you wish to make several small drums, use the cardboard tube on which new carpeting is rolled. Measure ten-inch lengths and cut these with a saw.

The material you use for the membrane should be elastic enough to expand a little when under tension. Rawhide or chamois are among the best materials. Sheet rubber one-sixteenth of an inch thick or the rubber of an old tire inner tube is also good. Heavy plastic that is strong, yet flexible, can be used if the drummer does not beat too hard on it.

If the body of your drum is metal, it will be difficult to attach the membrane to the body. You cannot use nails, tacks and such fasteners. But you could cover both ends. A can opener can be used to remove the bottoms of cans, canisters, etc. Some kind of lacing can be used to weave back and forth from top to bottom.

Cut the material for the cover(s) so that each one overlaps the opening by two inches. Soak animal skin—rawhide, chamois, etc.—in water until it is pliable. Poke holes or make them with a paper punch a half-inch in from the edge and about two inches apart all around the cover. If both ends of the drum are being covered, use rawhide strips or strong twine, and lace back and forth from the top head to the bottom. If you use a plastic covering, you may cover the whole drum. A large plastic bag can be drawn down, pulled under the drum body and twisted to tighten. A piece of cord can be tied around the twist.

If the body of the drum is of wood or heavy cardboard, you need cover only one end. Cut the material to overlap the opening by two inches, and soak animal skin until it is flexible. Tack it with two or three upholsterers' tacks close together on one side. Pull the material tight across the opening to the opposite side and secure it with two or three more tacks. Work in a square, pulling the material to the third side and securing it, then to the fourth side. Use as many tacks as necessary, keeping them no more than an inch apart.

Drums can be tapped with the fingers or beat with the fingers flat. Rhythm sticks can be used for beaters as long as the player is careful not to poke them through the membrane. Otherwise, a padded mallet makes the best beater. Usually one beater is used. (The snare drum is played with two sticks, one in each hand. There is a special technique required in using them.) During periods of rest the player should hold the head of the mallet in the free hand.

A drum can be used to suggest rhythmic body activities. It can be played in walk rhythm, run rhythm, skip rhythm, for slow walking, etc. Listeners hearing its "commands" can respond. It is indispensable for marching. A drum can imitate a ball bouncing, a truck dumping a heavy load, a rabbit thumping, someone walking in heavy boots, a door slamming, etc. The music of various peoples—the American Indians, Africans, Orientals, South Americans, islanders—requires that some kind of drum be played.

Have 4 large (twelve-inch diameter or more) drums, 1 minimum.

Have 8 small (six- to eleven-inch diameter) drums, 4 minimum.

Drumsticks. You will need drumsticks or mallets not only for playing drums, but also to tap cymbals to make them sound like gongs.

The handle of a drumstick can be a piece of half-inch dowel ten to twelve inches long. Cover the striking end of the dowel with a small wad of cotton batting. Secure it to the dowel with adhesive tape. Keep on winding tape over the cotton until it is completely covered. Add more cotton and again cover it with adhesive. Continue to build up the end with layers of cotton and tape until there is a bulge about a half-inch thick all around. By padding the head of the mallet you will give it resilience so that it will bounce off the drum head.

The mallet head should be covered with a piece of leather— leftover rawhide, chamois, etc. Cut the material in a circle, about six inches in diameter. Use a string or very heavy thread; take long stitches around the edge of the circle. Put this cover over the padding, pull the string or thread tight and tie it.

Make enough drumsticks for your gongs and drums.

Finger Cymbals. These small-sized cymbals can be purchased. They would be useful in interpreting some of the songs about China, about the desert, about Arabian dances, etc.

Gongs. A real gong is a large, dish-shaped, metal disc suspended on a rope fastened along the rim. Such a gong would have too powerful a sound in an ensemble of rhythm instruments. We suggest that in its stead a single large cymbal be used. It should be held horizontally by its handle and struck by a mallet.

The player prepares to play by keeping cymbal and mallet in front of him a few inches apart. The instrument can be played with a lot of force, or it can be tapped lightly. As soon as it has been played, the player should dampen the sound by holding the cymbal with the fingers of the hand holding the mallet.

A tap on a gong can be made to precede a drama of mystery. It suggests drama in the Orient and is often used in Chinese music. A gong struck with a metal striker (a spike or large nail) can be made to sound like a fire truck clanging. It can be used to imitate a blacksmith striking an anvil, church bells announcing a celebration, a building crashing, glass breaking, etc.

Jingle Sticks. A jingle stick, as the name suggests, consists of a stick for a handle and pieces of metal attached to the end, which make a jingling sound when the stick is shaken.

You can make a jingle stick using a piece of half-inch dowel about nine inches long for a handle. You will also need a wooden toy block one-and-a-half to two inches on a side, four to eight metal bottle caps, and six-penny common nails. (These are nails, one-and-a-half inches long, with heads.)

Drill holes in the centers of the bottle caps. The hole diameters should be slightly larger than the diameters of the nails so that the caps will be able to move freely on the nails when shaken. Drill a hole a half-inch in diameter into the center of one side of the toy block, going about one inch deep. Drive the dowel handle into the hole. Next, put two bottle caps onto a nail so that metal touches metal, and drive the nail at least half-way into the center of one side of the block. Put another set of bottle caps on the opposite side. Whether or not jingles are put on the other two sides of the block is optional.

It is possible to shake a jingle stick that has two sets of jingles opposite each other and get no sound. Children sometimes inadvertently do this, and you might need to show them how to shake the stick so the jingles make contact.

Jingle sticks can be used to imitate small bells; they sound like the jingle parts of tambourines. They can be played when the children sing songs about money jingling, about rain, about dancing in such cultures as those of gypsies, Italians, South Americans, people of the Middle Eastern countries, etc.

Have 12 jingle sticks, 4 minimum.

Maracas. Originally a maraca was a dried gourd with a hooked neck which was used for a handle. When it was shaken, the seeds inside rattled against the walls to make a swishing sound. Nowadays a maraca is usually a round or bulb-shaped rattle with pebbles or loose material inside.

A high-watt incandescent light bulb with a long neck that can serve as a handle can become a homemade maraca. Choose a burnt-out 75- or higher-watt bulb. This will be covered with papier-mache. Mix flour with a small amount of water, enough to make a wet paste. Tear newspaper into short strips about an inch wide and soak in the paste. Cover the bulb with a few layers of the wet paper strips, and set it aside until it is dry. Then very carefully give the bulb a few sharp raps at several places on the surface to break the glass inside. Try not to damage the papier-mache so that it keeps its bulb shape. Cover it with more layers of papier-mache to make it strong. When this has dried, the maraca can be painted with brightly colored designs.

Another method of making a maraca is to use a round balloon as a base. Blow it up to about the size of a baseball, and tie the end with a string. Then cover it with several layers of papier-mache, taking care not to cover the end. When it is dry, put a few rattles—small pebbles, dried rice, dried peas, bits of macaroni, etc.—into the opening. Then push a piece of half-inch dowel about nine inches long through the opening until it touches the inner surface of the balloon on the opposite side. Push a thumb tack through the papier-mache so that the point goes into the end of the dowel. Put glue around the handle at the point where it goes into the balloon. Then add more papier-mache to cover the glue and make the handle tight. When it is dry, the maraca is ready for decorating.

To play a maraca, hold it by the handle and shake. During periods of rest, the player should hold the bulb part of the instrument with his other hand to keep it still.

Maracas can be used to accompany Mexican dances, Latin and South American music, the calypso music of the West Indies, etc. Some of the American Indian tribes use a gourd rattle to accompany dances. The sound of a maraca is a little like that of rain.

Have 12 maracas, 4 minimum.

Rhythm Sticks. Some books refer to this instrument as "sticks." They are usually made of half-inch dowel. To make rhythm sticks, cut dowel in twelve-inch lengths, or, if you want to get more for your money, make them nine inches long. Sand the sharp edges on the ends. To finish them, you may stain with wood stain and varnish, paint with enamel paint, or leave them plain.

A player needs a pair of sticks, one for each hand. Young children may be tempted to tap their sticks, often without thinking, during periods when they are supposed to be quiet. Suggest that they keep them still by placing the ends of the sticks against the shoulders until just before time to play.

Rhythm sticks are perhaps the most used and the most useful rhythm instruments. They can sound like clocks ticking, train wheels clicking on tracks, a woodpecker tapping, knitting needles clicking, a carpenter hammering, a shoemaker tapping, someone knocking on a door, various kinds of machinery clacking, etc.

Have a dozen or more pairs of rhythm sticks, 6 pairs minimum.

Sand Blocks. This instrument consists of a pair of wooden blocks with handles. The bases have a sandpaper covering. A player holds a block in each hand and rubs the sanded surfaces together.

To make a pair of sand blocks, you will need two small blocks of wood. Use three-quarter-inch plywood cut approximately three by five inches, or cut one- by four-inch white pine into five-inch lengths. For a handle, use a scrap of lumber, a small empty thread spool, a small round drawer or cabinet handle, etc. Fasten one of these in the center of the back of each block with strong glue or with a flat-headed wood screw which is long enough to go most of the way through the wood block. If a screw goes through to the other side, the end can be filed off.

If you use regular sandpaper, it should be medium-grained. But, because sandpaper wears quickly and has a tendency to tear, it is better to use emery cloth which has a stronger backing and will last indefinitely. Cut the material into five- by five-inch pieces for each block (or make them a size that will allow an overlap of the edges of the block). Tack the material with carpet tacks spaced almost an inch apart along one long edge of a block. Make folds in it so that you can bring it across the underside and up along the opposite edge. Tack this side. Or, if you prefer, the material may be stapled with a staple "gun" along the edges. Then, strips of cloth seam binding can be glued over the staples. The blocks and handles can be painted, stained and varnished, or they can be left plain.

The player holds one sand block in each hand and rubs the rough surfaces against each other back and forth in rhythm.

Sand blocks can make sounds like various kinds of steam engines—a machine in a factory, a steam boat, a hissing train, etc. They can be used to imitate the sounds of a broom sweeping a floor, a saw sawing wood, roller skates, water splashing, etc.

Have 10 pairs of sand blocks, 4 pairs minimum.

Scrapers. The kind of scraper we have in mind is a rhythm stick which has been notched or fluted so that it gives a rough sound when something is stroked across it.

Older children can cut notches with wood carving tools along the length of pieces of half-inch dowel rhythm sticks. Younger children or those who might hurt themselves with cutting tools can scrape the wood with a small file or a rasp. Each scraper should have at least a half-dozen notches.

To play a scraper the person must hold it in one hand and stroke along its ridges with a smooth stick—a tongue depressor, a ruler, etc.—using a quick, sweeping motion.

The sound of a scraper can be frightening when it is made loud and suddenly, and it can be played with some Halloween songs. It can be used with songs about buzzing insects, crickets, etc. Scrapers are sometimes used to accompany Latin American music.

Have 10 scrapers, 4 minimum.

Shakers. The shaker is very similar to the maraca, except for a difference in tone because of the different materials used.

To make shakers, collect a variety of small receptacles with covers that can be fastened. Possibilities include a metal Bandaid box, a wooden or cardboard safety match box, a celluloid or plastic soap dish, and a small baby food jar with a screw top. If a glass jar is used, cover it completely with colored decorators' adhesive tape. The tape will keep the glass from shattering should the jar slip from a child's hand and break.

You should also have on hand several different shaker materials. The possibilities include rice, money, dried lentils, peas, beans, large dried seeds, small pebbles, larger pebbles, and elbow macaroni. Encourage the children to experiment by putting different materials into different containers and taking note of the sounds. Ask them to think of other experiments. It should occur to them to try fewer materials, then a lot. They could try larger- and smaller-sized materials and listen for the difference.

Because the shakers have no handles, they must be held in the hand and shaken to play. They can be used to accompany the same music as the maracas.

Have 10 shakers, 4 minimum.

Tambourines. By definition, a tambourine is a small drum that is held in the hand. Metal discs are inserted into holes in the rim, and these jingle when the drum head is hit or when the instrument is shaken.

Because it would be difficult to duplicate the manufactured instrument, it is recommended that you purchase two or more tambourines if you think you will find them useful.

A tambourine without jingles can be made from a pair of embroidery hoops and one or two sheets of durable plastic. This will work well, provided the player does not puncture the plastic or loosen it by hitting it too hard. Cut the plastic, the drum head material, an inch-and-a-half larger than the hoop size. The plastic must fit tight, so tight that the top hoop has to be forced onto the bottom. If they are loose, line the inside of the hoop without the felted surface with sticky tape. Use tape that does not have a smooth surface—masking tape, adhesive tape, etc.

There are two possible operations of a real tambourine. For one, it can be held in one hand and hit with the other. For the other, it can be shaken. The player must make sure when he shakes it that the instrument is held so that the jingles strike each other. You may need to help little children learn this.

A tambourine can be used by a dancer as part of his dance. It can also be played for such activities as whirling and twirling like snowflakes or leaves falling.

Have 6 tambourines, 2 minimum.

Triangles. The triangle got its name from its shape. If you straightened one out, you would find that it is a steel rod about fifteen inches long. When the rod is bent to form a triangle, one side will have a break. A loop of string or other holder must be attached so that the metal can be suspended for playing.

A solid-metal curtain rod, two to three feet long, can sound almost exactly like a commercially-produced triangle. Long rods can be cut to shorter lengths with a hacksaw. At one end of the rod, wind three or more thicknesses of electricians' or another type of sticky tape. Tie a string on the rod just under the tape for a holder. The tape will keep it from slipping off the rod. Use a large nail or a spike for a striker.

If you cannot get a steel rod like a curtain rod, use a long, heavy spike for a "triangle." Tie a string under the head to serve as a holder, and use another spike for a striker.

The player of a triangle must always hold it by a string or other holder if the tone is to sound resonant. During periods of rest the player can hold the metal with the fingers of the hand that holds the striker; this will prevent anyone from accidentally striking it at the wrong time.

The triangle can be used during the singing of songs about twinkling stars, icicles, dripping water, rain, etc. It can imitate a clock chiming the hour.

Have 8 triangles and strikers, 4 minimum.

Wood Blocks. The wood block, or tone block, makes a sound similar to claves. The instrument consists of a block of wood that has been hollowed out and a stick or mallet for a striker. The hollow sound is louder than the claves', and you may want to purchase a few to give your rhythm ensemble a variety of sound. Wood blocks can be used in the same way as claves.

USING RHYTHM INSTRUMENTS

You have made or bought a number of rhythm instruments for your class, and now it is time to try them. At some times you will want to have everyone playing an instrument. At other times you will need one or a few instruments to accompany a song, an activity, or perhaps a piece of orchestral music.

After you have set up a system for storing the instruments, inform the children about where they can find each one. Teach them the names of the instruments. Train them to go quietly to the storage area, get the instrument they are going to play, and return to their places. All children playing one instrument should sit together in a block. When you assign children, keep this in mind and assign everyone in an area to play the same instrument.

If necessary, teach the players how to play their instruments. Explain how they should be held during periods of rest—rhythm sticks and claves against the shoulders; bells, triangles, cymbals, jingle sticks, etc., held by both hands to keep them still. When they have finished playing, the children should return their instruments to their storage places.

Preliminary Exercises with Rhythm Instruments

An exercise like the following one can be used with groups of any age to help them become familiar with instruments. Little practice should be needed in playing since most rhythm instruments are easy to play. Tell the children that they will be given chances to play alone and with others. They should refrain from playing until time to do so.

Start the exercise by telling the children that people's first and last names can be spoken in rhythm, and that the natural rhythms can make interesting patterns. Every one of the following names, for instance, makes a different rhythmical pattern:

Lynn Rich - ard-son, | Pe-ter Mac-Car-thy, | Ev-e-lyn James, | Vin-cent

Rob-erts,   Ger-al - dine Jo-seph-son,   Ma-ry Anne Syl-ves-ter.

Ask half of the class on one side of the room to keep time. They should lightly clap a steady beat. Everyone else will take turns speaking their names in rhythm. You can point to the person whose turn it is and help those who need it. The half of the class that kept time should have a chance to say their names in rhythm while the others clap lightly for them.

Next, have the clapping stopped. Go around the room again, and see if everyone can still speak his name in rhythm. Review this part of the exercise as needed.

Divide the room into instrumental sections. If the children are very young, have two sections—those who play instruments made of wood and those who play instruments made of metal. Older children can be divided into four or more groups. One could be the group which plays instruments that ring; a second could have instruments that are tapped; a third instruments that swish; a fourth might play instruments that crash (cymbals), boom (drums), or click (castanets and scrapers). The children get the instruments themselves, guided by your descriptions.

Choose children from each group, to stand with their instruments in front of the class. Suggest a routine. For a "warm-up" have the first of these children speak his name in rhythm, then play it on his instrument, then everyone in his group play the same rhythm. The second child would do the same and his group would respond, and so on, until all have had a turn.

Next, the children whose names are being played in rhythm stand in front of their groups as leaders. (The children of the groups must watch their leaders and stay with them.) In this exercise everyone must think the child's name in rhythm and play it on their instruments when you signal. You could do this by holding a hand over the heads of the leaders, one after another. If there are only two children, repeat the exercise a few times. Hold your hands over the heads of two leaders at a time, and have both rhythms of the two names played together.

Ostinato Exercises with Rhythm Instruments

The following exercises are similar to the preliminary exercises above, except that, instead of having the players think of a person's name which is only one measure long, they will be thinking of a descriptive sentence about an instrument which will be two measures long and which can be repeated like an ostinato.

First, choose instruments which will make a variety of rhythms. The rhythms of some sentences below are fast, some are slow, some move along evenly, some are uneven, some have more rests than others, etc. As soon as you have decided which instruments to use, write descriptive sentences about them on the chalk board. Use the following, or have the children make up their own.

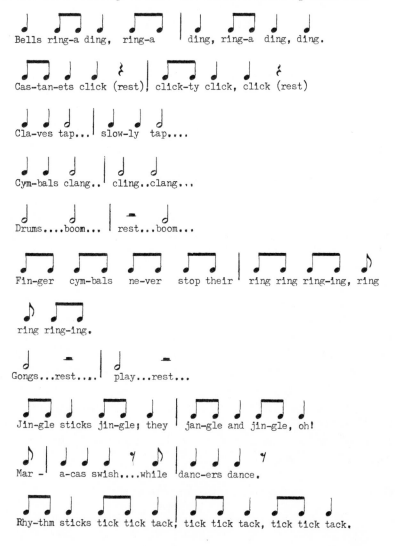

Bells ring-a ding, ring-a | ding, ring-a ding, ding.

Cas-tan-ets click (rest)| click-ty click, click (rest)

Cla-ves tap...| slow-ly tap....

Cym-bals clang..| cling..clang...

Drums....boom...| rest...boom...

Fin-ger cym-bals ne-ver stop their | ring ring ring-ing, ring

ring ring-ing.

Gongs...rest....| play...rest...

Jin-gle sticks jin-gle; they | jan-gle and jin-gle, oh!

Mar -| a-cas swish....while |danc-ers dance.

Rhy-thm sticks tick tick tack| tick tick tack, tick tick tack.

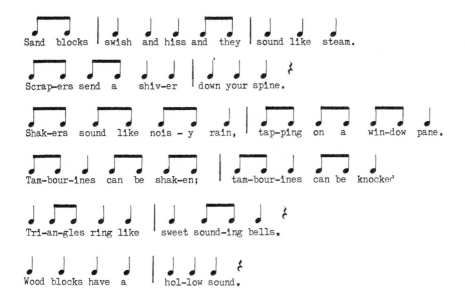

Sand blocks swish and hiss and they sound like steam.

Scrap-ers send a shiv-er down your spine.

Shak-ers sound like nois - y rain, tap-ping on a win-dow pane.

Tam-bour-ines can be shak-en; tam-bour-ines can be knocked

Tri-an-gles ring like sweet sound-ing bells.

Wood blocks have a hol-low sound.

While you point to the words of each sentence on the board, everyone should chant them in rhythm. When the children are able to speak them well, have them get the instruments they are to play. This time, when you point to a sentence, the group that is playing the instrument should speak the sentence in rhythm, then play the rhythm while thinking the words.

As a next step, point to the sentences again. This time, the players of the particular instrument a sentence describes should respond by playing the rhythm while thinking the words.

You are now ready to have everyone do the rhythms in a kind of improvised composition. Tell the children that they are to play their rhythms when you signal them to start, and they are to keep going until you show them with a hand signal that they are to stop.

Signal the players of one of the slower-moving instruments, like claves, drums, gongs, etc., to start. As soon as they are well established and seem sure of their rhythm, bring in a second instrument. If both of those groups are going well, have the third group join them, then the fourth, etc., until everyone is playing. Next, signal the group that came in last to stop. Work backward, signaling groups to stop until only the first players are left. If they play the last note softly, it can make for a very effective ending.

Encourage the children to experiment with different instruments, bringing them in in different orders. Older children can take your place as leaders of these improvisations.

Playing the Rhythms of Songs in Round or Canon Form

In this exercise the children will play familiar songs on their instruments. They will play the rhythm of the words in the form of a round or canon. The song chosen need not be a round, since no harmony will be heard and only rhythms will be expressed. However, not all songs work well, and the song chosen should have phrases with a variety of rhythms. A song like 'She'll Be Comin' 'Round the Mountain" would be a poor choice because the rhythms of each phrase are almost exactly the same. Everyone moves along in eighth-note rhythm until the word "comes" which is always held.

A good song choice, among others, is "Row, Row, Row Your Boat" which begins with notes that "walk" along, that "skip" up to the word "stream," which is held. The third phrase—"Merrily, merrily, merrily, merrily"—moves quickly, and the fourth phrase repeats the rhythm of the second phrase. In this song, then, there are three different rhythms in the four phrases.

To present a lesson, have younger children perform each step in the procedure at least once. Older and more capable children may be able to skip some of the easier steps.

1. Everyone sings the song.
2. The song is sung again, and the rhythm of the words is clapped during the singing.
3. Everyone thinks the words without singing and claps his rhythm.
4. Assign blocks of children to play certain instruments. After everyone has his instrument, have the rhythm of the words played on all instruments together.
5. Divide the class in half. Have each half play the rhythm of the words. When they do it well, have the two groups play it as a round. Start Group 1, and when they are about to start the second phrase, bring in Group 2.
6. If Step 5 has gone well, make more divisions. As one section, you might have the tappers; the shakers could be a second section, crashers and boomers a third, jinglers a

fourth, etc. One group starts. When they get to the second phrase or measure, signal a second group to start. When they reach the same place, signal the third, etc. If the song is short, have it repeated.

Playing Songs Using Three Different Rhythms

In the previous exercises, instruments were used to play the rhythm of words—people's names, descriptive phrases about the rhythm instruments, and, finally, the words of songs. In this exercise, the instruments will be used to play three kinds of rhythms for a song—the rhythm of the words, the underlying beat, and the first beat of every measure.

This should be an easy exercise for any group. It is not necessary to give the children any written reminders, but to show you how the three rhythms will fit together, here is an example. If the notes to be played on the first phrase of "Oh, Susanna" were written out, this is how they would look:

1. Rhythm of the words

2. Rhythm of the beat

3. First beat of each measure

After children have had experience with playing songs in this way, they will be able to help choose instruments. For the first few times, you should suggest what should be used on each part. Have the word players use instruments that are easy to manipulate, because their rhythms will be the most demanding. The players who keep the beat should use instruments that make a distinct sound— rhythm sticks, claves, etc., rather than instruments like bells or maracas which sound less clear. Those who play the first beat of every measure may use an accent instrument, like the drums, gongs or cymbals.

The playing should start with the instruments that are to keep the beat. Once they have established a steady rhythm, bring in the instruments that play the first beats of measures. Finally, signal the players who play the rhythm of the words. If the song is short, have them play it twice through. After they have finished, signal the players who are keeping the beat to stop. Let those who play the first beat of each measure play the last note.

ACCOMPANYING WITH RHYTHM INSTRUMENTS

So far, we have discussed some of the ways to use rhythm instruments by themselves. There will be times when the instruments can be used to accompany other music. Oftentimes, the songs in the children's books will sound better with the addition of the sound of a few rhythm instruments. Specific suggestions are sometimes made by the writers of the books, but it may be you and your children who will recognize that a song needs embellishment. If you refer back to the paragraphs describing the instruments starting on page 166, you will find notes about some of the principal uses of each one.

Rhythm instruments can also be used to accompany orchestral music. When this is done throughout a whole composition, the instruments are called a rhythm band.

Using Rhythm Instruments to Accompany Songs

Usually, only a few instruments are played during the singing of a song. The singing is featured, and most children will sing, not play. The playing may be needed only in a few places.

Many, if not most, children's songs would be spoiled by the addition of rhythm instruments. The song that has its own intrinsic beauty and the song that is more melodic or harmonic than rhythmic should have no accompaniment. But, there are songs about the dances and music of other countries that sound better with instruments. Songs about circuses, bands, parades, etc., should never be sung without a rhythm instrument accompaniment. The counting songs of young children could have a different instrument played whenever a number was sung. You will find other uses for several different instruments in single songs.

But most songs will call for one or two types of instrument. The singing of "Jingle Bells," for instance, could be enriched by the addition of jingle sticks, bells or triangles. A song about trotting horses would need the sounds of some kind of instrument that imitates hoofs hitting the ground—perhaps claves, wood blocks, or rhythm sticks. Maracas and shakers would remind listeners of the sounds of rain; sand blocks could sound like a train starting; scrapers and shakers could be used to make a Halloween song sound scary;

rhythm sticks or wood blocks could sound like the ticking of a clock, and a gong could be used to strike the hours.

Before you suggest to your class that they think of an instrumental accompaniment for a song, be sure they know the music well. You may find that if you ask for opinions from young children as to what instruments should be used, they will suggest only instruments that they like and want to play. They may also suggest that they play throughout the whole piece, not because it would sound well, but because it would give them a feeling of prestige. To circumvent this, let the children take turns at playing the instruments and being the singers. The singers will make judgments about which instruments to use, how many there should be, when they should play, etc. The players will know that they will not play an instrument for the songs on which they are the singers.

You can prepare for a lesson in which rhythm instruments will be chosen to accompany a song by putting a few of the instruments where they can be seen by everyone. There could be one or two of each kind that would be suitable for the particular song. Ask the children to think about the instruments while they are singing the song.

When the singing is over, ask the judges to name one instrument which they think would sound well with that particular song. How should the instrument be played? When should it come in? After a discussion, have the suggestions tried. Next, ask for comments about the results. Do the judges think there should be more or less notes played? Should more or fewer instruments be used?

Ask the judges if any other instruments would sound well with this song. Discuss the suggestions, and try the best. Make revisions to suit the judges' tastes. When definite decisions have been made, help the children write a score.

Suppose, for example, the song chosen for rhythm instrument accompaniment is "Home on the Range." You would prepare for the lesson by putting instruments on display. Because it is a cowboy song and the rhythm suggests a cowboy's horse trudging slowly, you would have instruments like claves, drums, rhythm sticks, and wood blocks in view. You might also have a triangle and a gong, since on a ranch various kinds of bells are used to call people to dinner or to have them assemble. Instruments like the maracas or shakers and sand blocks could be included if your group is older or more capable, and they might want to add a sound effect something like wind rustling leaves. Younger children should have only a few instruments to choose from.

You should guide the children by asking them if they can think of an ostinato accompaniment. Which instrument could play the steady beats, which play the accents or first beats of each measure, and which might play the rhythm of the words? If they want an ostinato, it can be a rhythm found in one or two of the words. The word "buffalo" in the second phrase, for instance, has an uneven rhythm which could be repeated throughout the song. The steady beats could be played by an instrument which sounds like a horse walking; and the accents could be played by an instrument that sounds like the gong used on ranches to call people together.

Writing a Music Score for Rhythm Instruments

A music score, like any other written message, exists to give people a reminder of whatever it is they want to remember. You and your children can invent a method of making a record of what you decide to do on rhythm instruments in a piece of music. Or you can use the conventional notation system.

Most scores for songs will have rhythm patterns that are repeated throughout the singing of the song. It is easy to make a small score for one or two measures. If the song is "Home on the Range," for example, maracas might play an ostinato, rhythm sticks could play the steady beat that sounds like walking, a drum could play the accents or first beats of measures. The score would look like this:

It should be easy to express what you want rhythm instruments to do using the conventional notation system. However, you may occasionally need to invent a way of showing a special way of playing. To show that an instrument like bells, maracas, jingle sticks, or shakers is to be shaken, make the note that shows the length of time. Then make crosses on the stem, like this: ♩ or ♪ ,etc. When a tambourine is to be shaken, you could use this sign: ♩ When it is to be tapped, use this: ♪

If drums are to be played with two sticks, one in each hand, show that a note is for the left hand by having the stem go down: ♩ A note to be played by the stick in the right hand will have the stem going up: ♩.

If only two instruments are to be played, and if the note patterns are not complicated, put them on the same line with the stems for one instrument going up, the other going down:

Rhythm Sticks: ♩♩♩♩♩♩♩♩
Drum:

Using Rhythm Instruments to Accompany Orchestral Music

There are a few orchestral pieces which sound well when accompanied by rhythm instruments. During the playing of a march on a record player, for instance, every kind of rhythm instrument could be played. While they listened to the music, the children could decide when to bring in each instrument. Usually, the loudest instruments would be played very little, perhaps on the first beat of every measure. Those instruments that are moderately loud would be played when the music on the recording was strongest. And the softest instruments would be played when the music was soft.

Some of the waltzes of Johann Strauss would sound well with the addition of rhythm instruments. You and your children could make an arrangement which would include every child in the class and most of the different kinds of instruments. Other dance music, especially for Spanish, Latin American and West Indian dances, can be accompanied by maracas, shakers, drums, castanets, claves, wood blocks, as well as other rhythm instruments.

A few recordings are available of selected musical compositions suited for accompaniment by a rhythm band. Music like "Amaryllis" by Ghys and "Rendezvous" by Aletter in the album, "Rhythm Bands," part of the RCA Victor Basic Record Library for Elementary Schools, and "The Changing of the Guard" from Bizet's "Carmen Suite" or Grieg's "In the Hall of the Mountain King," both in "Adventures in Music" Grade 3, Volume II, are recommended.

Chapter 6

YOU CAN TEACH MELODY-PLAYING

ON INSTRUMENTS

Every melody is formed so as to have a rhythmic pattern. It is dependent on a set of notes called a scale. Each note selected to form a melody has harmony understood, and these harmonies must make a satisfying progression which ends on the primary chord of the scale used. This is called the tonic chord.

The person who plays a melody on a musical instrument is required to play it in a prescribed rhythm, and he must know how to make changes in pitch on the instrument in order to play the sequence of notes that is needed. He is also supposed to produce pleasant-sounding tones. If he is to perform all these tasks with efficiency, the instrument player should probably have training. To gain skill he may need to practice with his instrument in frequent sessions over a long period of time.

The job of learning to play a melody instrument like a violin, a piano, a French horn or a bassoon can be arduous. Luckily, there are simpler instruments on which anyone can make a pleasing tone with little effort. The job of playing melodies can be simplified if only a few different notes are used and if the rhythmic patterns are not complicated. Even a teacher who has never played a melody instrument himself can teach melody-playing on instruments.

There are three chief methods of making sound with definite pitch. One is to vibrate a length of wire or string that is under tension; a second is to use wind to cause a column of air inside a wooden or metal tube to vibrate; and the third is to make vibrations by striking some object such as a bar of metal or wood.

The chief instruments of an orchestra are represented by these three ways of making sounds of definite pitch. In the string section, the instruments have wire or catgut strings, and their sounds are amplified by the sound chamber across which they are stretched. They are vibrated by being plucked or scraped with the strings of a bow. In the wind sections—the brass and woodwind—vibrations are set up when the player forces air into the pipe or tube. And in the percussion section of the orchestra, the metal or wooden bars of the instruments are suspended to keep them away from any material that might damp the vibrations. A mallet is used to strike the bars and cause them to vibrate. When you teach students to make sound, you can help them understand each method.

To make the variety of tones needed in a melody, each type of instrument can be made to change pitch in its own way. The piano has eighty-eight previously-tuned strings which are sounded at the player's discretion by a hammer mechanism for each string. The violin, on the other hand, also is a stringed instrument, but it has only four strings. To change the pitch of a string the player shortens its length by pressing it with his finger and holding it on a board at the proper point.

Changes in pitch in the tube-type wind instrument are accomplished by making air go longer or shorter distances. To produce the lowest-sounding note possible, the air must go the longest distance. In the wind instrument, the tube has holes, and the player must cover all of them to make the lowest note. In the brass instrument, there are extra lengths of tube through which the air is forced to pass, either by diverting it with valves or by extending the tube. To produce high-sounding notes, holes are left uncovered on the woodwind pipes; tube lengths are shortened on the brass.

To change pitch on a bar-type percussion instrument, the player strikes the bars of shorter length to make higher sounds and those of longer length to get lower sounds.

While it is important that an instrument player spend time learning only on an instrument that sounds well and functions well, it is also important to avoid feeling that only instruments con-structed like present-day orchestral instruments are worthy. A California scientist suggests that instruments could probably be successfully made from a variety of materials. He has made a good, mellow-toned clarinet from a piece of five-eighths-inch plastic garden hose. He learned from this experiment that the bell (the fluted part at the end of a typical clarinet) was unnecessary.

The pages of this chapter will tell you ways in which you will be able to help your children experiment with making instruments that make tones of definite pitch and on which melodies can be played. You will also be told how to teach students to play simple melody instruments, including percussion instruments using some of the Orff techniques.

MAKING MELODY WITH STRINGS

The stringed instruments of the orchestra—violin, viola, 'cello, bass, and harp—sound pleasant to our ears, probably because their tones remind us of the tones of human voices. Many composers have written string quartets and trios, long compositions for these instruments alone.

Stringed instruments are popular, but it usually takes years of study and practice to learn to play one well. The player must get the knack of making a pleasing tone. He must know how to find the exact places on the strings where he will get the pitches he wants, and he must do it with great accuracy.

You will not be teaching children to play such instruments, but with them you can try easy experiments to help them discover how pitch can be changed with a tightly stretched band. Older children can construct a single-stringed instrument that has some of the characteristics of the stringed members of an orchestra.

Learning about Stringed Instruments

To teach children about the vibrations of strings you can use large rubber bands, books and rulers. With older children slightly more elaborate experiments can be done with boxes for sound chambers, rubber bands and rulers.

Before presenting a lesson at any grade level, try to pique the children's interest by having them watch someone play a stringed instrument or hear one played on a recording. Ask questions about what they have seen or heard. How is the instrument played? What is the player's "stick" called? The stringed player's "bow" is made with the long white hairs from a horse's tail. These are fastened to a stick and pulled tight so that they scrape the strings and make them vibrate when pulled across them. Sometimes the player plucks the strings; he pulls one out a little way and lets it go. Harp strings are played by plucking.

Experiments for Lower Grades. Suggest to the children that you make a stringed instrument with a rubber band. Use a wide band large enough to fit around a book. Put it on the book, and have someone pluck it to see if it makes a musical sound. (It will probably snap back onto the book with a thud.) Ask if anyone knows how a real musical instrument is constructed to allow a plucked string to make a pleasing sound. Someone may have noticed that an instrument like a violin has its strings raised a little by a small, thin piece of wood. This is called the bridge. Suggest that a ruler pushed under the band and turned on its edge will raise the rubber band nicely.

Have someone pluck the rubber band after it has been raised. It will vibrate freely and should make sound of a definite pitch. Have the tone lightly hummed by the children. Ask them if anyone knows a way to make the pitch of the band higher. Try whatever is suggested. If no one can think of a workable solution, hint that high-sounding instruments are small and their strings are short. How could the rubber band be shortened using the ruler? (Without tipping it over, move the ruler closer to the edge of the book.) Have someone pluck the shortened length of rubber, and have everyone hum the pitch. Let children take turns moving the ruler back or forth. Each time it is moved, the band should be plucked, and the tone should be hummed. Have the children formulate a rule for what they are doing.

Do the children know how the instrument player shortens a string to make the pitch higher? The same can be done with the rubber band. It can be pressed with the hand against the book at a spot in from the edge. While it is held, the shortened band should be plucked and the tone produced hummed. The person's hand should be removed, the band plucked again, and the lower tone hummed. After a number of trials, the children should discuss what they have been doing and formulate a rule.

Does anyone know how the violin player raises the pitch of a string before he starts to play? He tightens it by turning the peg to which it is attached. Can anyone think of a way to tighten the rubber band? Someone might think of pulling the ruler out a little way from the book; someone else might think of increasing the thickness of the book by adding to it; someone else might suggest putting the rubber band around a larger book, etc.

If possible, at the conclusion of these experiments, have a player of a stringed instrument demonstrate it to the children. He should start by tuning the instrument in front of the children, tightening and loosening strings while plucking them. Ask a child to explain what he is doing. The player should play a short tune on one string only, and a child should talk about the changes in pitch and how they were made. Finally, the player should play a melody using all of the strings. Ask a child to make comments.

Experiments for Upper Grades. For these experiments you will need an empty box like a cardboard stationery box, a child's shoe box, or any small, sturdy box which could serve as a sound chamber. Seal it by putting masking tape over all cracks and holes and taping on the cover. Put a large rubber band around the whole box and let someone pluck it. Ask the children if the sound is musical. If not, what can they suggest to improve it. Someone should suggest that the band be raised to allow it to vibrate freely when plucked. Use a ruler turned on edge to hold the rubber band away from the box. When it is plucked while in this position, the band should make a more musical sound.

Point out to the children that the "box" part of a violin, a guitar or any other stringed instrument is its sound chamber. What is done to these boxes to allow the sound to escape? (One or more holes are cut in the top.) What happens in real instruments is that the vibrations of the strings as they are being played cause the sound chamber box to vibrate also, thus making the sound louder. With a knife, cut a hole about two to three inches in diameter in the top of your box. It need not be round. The rubber band should be plucked again; its tone should sound less muffled. Ask everyone to hum the tone they hear.

Ask the children to think of ways to make the pitch of the string higher. They should remember that the stringed instrument player tunes each string with a peg which makes it tighter so that it sounds higher. Have them show you ways to tighten the rubber band. (The ruler could be pulled out and away from the box; the band could be pulled away from the box by a finger; something could be added to the box, etc.) Have the new tone hummed.

Tightening the string is one method of raising its pitch. Can the children name another? What does the stringed instrument player do with his fingers to raise the pitch of the strings? Older children should tell you that he presses his fingers on the strings to make them touch the finger board and thus to shorten their length. Have them think of at least two methods of shortening the rubber band. One might be to press the string against the box with the fingers; a second could be to move the ruler closer to the edge of the box. Each time a higher tone is produced, the rubber band should be plucked and the pitch of it hummed.

Ask the children if they would know how to play a melody on a rubber-band instrument. Name a song of few notes like "Merrily We Roll Along" ("Mary Had a Little Lamb"), "Hot Cross Buns," "Old MacDonald," etc. Assign someone who has volunteered to practice in privacy (a corner of the room, a separate room, the hall corridor, etc.). At the next lesson he should play the song for the class. Other volunteers may take turns finding tunes.

Making and Playing a Stringed Instrument

The stringed instrument that has four or more strings must be kept tuned because each string must relate to the others if the player is to play a sequence of notes. Accurate tuning is necessary for successful playing; this is a task which requires skill.

It is less important to keep a single-stringed instrument tuned. If the one string were to loosen and the pitch drop a little, the change would hardly be noticeable. A big problem for the multi-stringed player is that each of his strings is tuned to a different pitch, and he must know how to move unhesitatingly from one to another to play a melody. It is far less difficult to find a melody on a single-stringed instrument.

If you elect to have your children make and learn to play a single-stringed instrument, they will learn how the tuning peg functions, putting tension on the string; how much force to use to hold the string against the finger board; how to space the fingers to get the desired intonations; how to give the instrument support in order to play it. Those who make their own instruments will become aware of the importance of the sound box as a resonance chamber, the use of a bridge to support strings and allow them to vibrate freely, as well as other reasons for construction features.

The single-stringed instruments which are available for purchase are not well-known and are generally not easy to find. Something called a monolin has a single string, while the duobass (distributed by Peripole) and the two-string ukelele or Pianolin have two strings.

One ready-made single-string instrument is called the gusle and comes from Yugoslavia. Its wooden body is shaped like half of a scooped-out pear and is about six inches high. The opening is covered with calf skin. The neck is about ten inches long and extends away from the body. The string is attached to the base of the instrument, crosses a bridge, passes along the finger board and is secured by the tuning peg. There is a bow made of an arched piece of wood about twelve inches long with a handle on the end. The bow strings are attached and hooked to a notch below the handle, and this makes it look something like a hunter's bow.

You can help your children make a single-stringed instrument. Call it a monochord. (Mono- in Greek means "single" plus chordē which means "string.") You will need a sounding box with one or more holes in the top. (The f-shaped sound holes in the top of a violin are of a certain size, and the size helps determine the pitch at which the air in the box will resonate.) Find a cigar box or other thin wooden box about six by nine inches and two inches deep. Remove the cover and carefully drill one or more holes in it. Leave the cover off to facilitate nailing, etc.

The neck of the monochord can be a piece of one- by two-inch pine twelve to fourteen inches long. Use a piece of half-inch dowel two-and-a-half inches long for a tuning peg. Drill two small (nail-size) holes across the two ends of the dowel about a half-inch in from each end. The hole on one end will hold a short nail which will act as a handle for turning the peg. The string will pass through the other small hole.

Use a seven-sixteenth inch drill bit to make a hole for the tuning peg. It should be an inch or more from the end of the neck piece and in the center of the two-inch side. Enlarge the hole a little by rolling the bit around the edges while the drill is running. The half-inch dowel tuning peg must fit tightly against the wall of the hole so that the peg will slip as little as possible after tuning. Insert the peg in the hole. The hole for the string will be above the neck; the hole for the nail handle will be below.

Use a bracket to attach the neck to the sounding box. This could be a piece of one- by two-inch wood about three inches long. Just for a moment put the box cover on so you can see how to attach the bracket. It should be centered against one of the short sides of the box and should be level with the top of the cover. Remove the cover and attach the bracket with glue and wood screws.

On the other end of the box put a piece of wood of three-quarter-inch material long enough to fit up and down the width of the side. Glue it to the middle. Drive a small screw or nail into the block; let it protrude a little so the string can be attached.

Make a bridge from three-quarter-inch wood two inches long. Cut a slender groove across the middle where the string will cross; this will help keep the string in place. Place the bridge near the end where the string will be fastened, just in front of the hole on the cover. Use glue and small nails or screws. Carefully glue the cover to the box. Place the neck onto the cover so that the end of the wood comes close to the edge of the hole. Glue it to the cover and the bracket. Screw it to the bracket for extra strength.

Violin strings are made of thin metal, of pig gut, or of gut wound with fine silver or aluminum wire. Purchase one of the thinner-sized, perhaps an A string, from a musical instrument supply store. Tie the end of the string to the nail or screw at the bottom of the sound box; bring it up across the bridge and down the finger board to the hole in the tuning peg. Insert the end through the hole. Leave three inches of excess and cut the rest. (If possible, cut the string in half so you can use the other half.)

Hold the string carefully, and bring it back out of the hole until only an inch is protruding. Keep holding it firmly with one hand while turning the peg with the other, making the string form a coil around the top of the peg. Keep pressure on the string until the winding is completed.

Tune the string to middle C. Play the note on the piano and pluck the string. Tighten or loosen the peg until the sounds are matched. The string will drop in pitch until it is conditioned, and you may want to re-tune it frequently. However, accurate tuning is not important unless the monochord is to be played with other instruments.

There are various ways to support a stringed instrument. Ask the children to describe them and tell why they think each is used. They should recognize that the violinist uses his chin to hold his instrument, leaving both arms and hands free for manipulating. The guitarist has a cord around his shoulders attached to his guitar; he also presses it against his abdomen with his arm while the fingers of the same hand strum the strings. The cellist rests the end of his instrument on the floor and rests it against his left knee. Have different children hold the monochord in various ways to try to find the best one. Eventually they will probably agree that holding the neck with the left hand while pressing the body of the instrument against the abdomen with the right will work best.

As a next step, locate the notes of the string. Use a piano to help you. The string itself must be tuned to middle C. At a point exactly halfway between the bridge and the end of the string you will find a pitch that sounds like the C that is an octave above middle C when you press the string against the neck. As soon as you have the correct spot, use a ruler to make a straight line across the neck; label it "C." If the children are capable, give them the job of locating the other notes in both octaves. They need to find both low and high D, E, F, G, A, and B. They should mark the locations lightly with a pencil. When they are finished, you should check each note as marked with the piano. If they are correctly located, write the letter names and draw the lines for each note using a pen, felt-tipped pen or other marking device. If there is room, add B$\flat$, the black note on the piano between A and B, and F#, the black note between F and G.

The string of the monochord can be plucked with the fingers or with a pick. To make a pick try different materials. For a strong tone use a coin. To get a different effect use a piece of plastic that has been cut from a detergent bottle. Try a piece of vinyl floor covering. Use an eraser for a soft sound.

Let the children take turns trying to find easy tunes by ear. They can work in their spare time in the music corner or other private area. As soon as each one is ready, have him give a demonstration to the class.

You can also give the children formal instruction on playing the monochord. Turn to the Song Section at the end of this chapter, and choose a song that is well known and that has few notes, something like "Merrily We Roll Along."

Instruct the player to hold the monochord horizontally in his lap, the string away from himself and his left hand under the neck. The thumb and palm of this hand will clasp the neck and hold it steady. The fifth finger should be held close to the G line, ready to press the string. The fourth finger should be at the F line, the third at E and the second at D. (No fingers will be needed to play middle C.) The heel of the player's right hand can be used to press the instrument against the abdomen to hold it steady; the thumb should be free to pluck the string.

The first note of "Merrily We Roll Along" is E. The player should press the string hard against the neck with the third finger of the left hand at the E line; at the same time he should pluck the string with a pick or with the thumb of his other hand. Then, without hesitation, he should press the string at the D line with the second finger of his left hand and pluck it with his right thumb (or pick). He must remove all fingers to play C, use the second finger to play D again, the third for E, and so forth.

Make a music staff and put the notes of the song being played on the chalk board. Write the letter names of the notes the first time they appear only. These should be written under the staff. For "Merrily We Roll Along" you would write E under the first note, D under the second, C under the third, and G under the twelfth. Ask different children to go to the board and write the letter names of the other notes. Explain that so-fa syllable names are used in singing and letter names for instrumental playing.

As soon as possible, the player of the monochord should train himself to find notes on the instrument by feeling for them. He will have to think to judge distances at first, and this will slow him down. But eventually he should appreciate the fact that he will be saving the time of shifting his eyes back and forth from the notes to the finger board on the neck. If players have trouble finding note places on the finger board by feel, use a pen knife or a wood carving tool to make fine grooves on the lines so they can be felt by the fingers.

When a player is playing a song or piece of music that uses more than the first five notes of the scale, he must re-position his left hand to reach the higher notes. If he is required only to play as high as the note A along with the lower notes, he will not need to shift the hand. But, if he is required to play higher notes—B, C, D, etc.—the whole hand should slide up to reach all of the higher notes to be played. The skilled player is able to shift rapidly back and forth from lower to higher positions so there is no break in the playing. Playing up and down the scale is a good means of practicing shifting and playing the notes without noticeable breaks.

MAKING MELODY BY BLOWING

Musical instruments which are made to sound by blowing must have enclosed space. A tube or pipe provides the player with such a space. He must blow into it to force the air against the walls of the pipe, causing the vibrations which are heard as musical sounds of definite pitch. The pitch depends on the size of the air chamber. The longer the pipe, the lower the pitch.

The wind instruments of the orchestra make sounds in various ways. In the flutes and piccolos vibrations are started when air hits the edge of the mouthpiece. The player blows across the opening in the way a person might blow air across the top of a bottle to give rise to vibrations. In a reed instrument like the clarinet, saxophone, oboe, bassoon, etc., the player's blowing causes the reed to vibrate; this in turn starts the vibration of air against the inner walls of the pipe. In the brass group—trumpet, trombone, French horn, tuba, etc.—the player tenses his lips and forces air through them to make them vibrate. These vibrations continue in the tube of the instrument.

A great deal of technical knowhow and much practice are needed for a person to produce a tone on most of these instruments. However, if you keep your experiments simple, you can lead your children to make sounds of definite pitch by blowing. And you can teach children of third grade and up to play a simple wind instrument.

Learning about Wind Instruments

Children can learn much about how wind instruments work by experimenting with having various amounts of air in bottles. The largest bottles are capable of producing the lowest sounds; the smallest make the highest. Any bottle's pitch can be raised by replacing some of its air with water. Children can learn about pitch; they can learn the technique of blowing across the bottle opening, a technique similar to the one used by the flute player.

Experiments for Lower Grades. You will need eight or more bottles of the same size. They must have small necks and small openings; wider-mouthed bottles like milk bottles cannot be used. Get bottles that are one-half pint to a quart in size. Try to get the kind with screw tops. Using the tops will prevent loss of water, either by evaporation or through spillage. You will also need a pitcher of water and a funnel.

If possible, motivate the first lesson by giving the children some kind of experience with wind instruments, either the experience of hearing someone play one or of hearing a recording that features a wind instrument. If they know the names of any instruments that are played by blowing, have them tell those they know. Ask questions about how sound is made in such instruments. Does anyone know how pitch is changed? (The player covers and uncovers holes in a woodwind instrument; the trombonist slides a long tube back and forth on an inside tube; all other brass players press valves to make the air travel longer distances.) Can anyone tell how the lowest note is made on an instrument with holes? (The player must cover all holes to make the air go the longest possible distance.) How is the highest note made? (All holes are left uncovered. Air goes as far as the first open hole.)

Hold up one of the empty bottles, and ask the children what is inside it. Someone will say there is only air. Tell them that you are going to blow carefully across the top of the bottle to force the air against the sides of the bottle. Ask them to listen for the vibrations. (Press the rim of the opening against your chin just under your lower lip and try to bring your upper lip over the top. Blow lightly. If necessary, adjust the position of the bottle until you are able to produce a tone.)

Tell the children that you would like to make a higher-pitched sound on the bottle, but it has no holes, no valves, no tubes—no apparent means for changing pitch. How can it be done? If no one has a suggestion, remind everyone of the purpose of the holes and tubes of wind instruments. (The purpose is to force the air to travel longer or shorter distances to make the pitch lower or higher.) Someone should tell you that the amount of air in the bottle will affect the pitch.

It is impossible to make holes in bottles. Ask if anyone can think of a way to lessen the amount of air in a bottle. Try to elicit the idea that putting something like water in the bottle will force the same amount of air out. Before trying this, ask the children to listen to the pitch of the empty bottle while you blow across the opening. Pour in a little water and blow again. Ask the children to tell you the difference in sound. Add a little more water and blow once more. Have a child tell what has been learned from the experiment.

Encourage the children to learn to make a musical tone by blowing across bottle tops in their spare time. Each child should have his own bottle to avoid spreading germs. If it should be necessary for different children to use the same bottle, teach them to clean the rim with a wad of cotton soaked in an antiseptic like a strong mouthwash, alcohol, etc. Also, caution them against blowing too much. They should practice for only a few seconds at a time; a session that goes on too long can cause the player to feel lightheaded.

Line up the eight bottles for the experiments. Ask the children to guess how they would sound if they were played. They should realize that they would all sound about the same. Have eight children who have practiced play the bottles by turns. Tell the class that you would like to make a scale with the eight bottles. They should recall the experiment in which the pitch of a bottle was changed by adding water to displace air.

Have the scale sung using the so-fa syllables. (If the scale names are not known, have the children learn them. Suggestions for teaching start on page 37.) Choose one of the eight bottles to be the sound of low "do." It will have no water and will be the lowest sounding. Make a label using letters about two inches high that can be seen clearly from the other side of the classroom. (Paste a label to the glass, tie a name tag to the neck, print with a felt-tipped marker, etc.)

Tell the children that you need them to help you make one of the bottles into "re." Have "do" played, and ask everyone to sing "do, re" and stop. "Re" should be sung again so that the pitch will be remembered. A second bottle should have a little water poured into it and its player should test the sound. If it is still too low, add more water. Continue adding and subtracting water as needed. Have "do, re" sung; have them played on the bottles. As soon as the "re" bottle is in tune, label it.

Continue to tune bottles to the notes of the scale in the same way. Choose a third bottle for "mi." Pour more water into it than is in the second bottle. Have the first two notes, "do, re," sounded on the two tuned bottles. Everyone should sing "do, re, mi" and repeat "mi." The player of the third bottle should blow across its top. The children should tell you if the sound is too high, too low, or just right. Make whatever adjustments are needed and label the bottle "mi."

You may stop tuning the bottles after you have located three notes if the children have tired of the procedure. It will be possible to play a few of the melodies from the Song Section at this time. (Use your discretion about dividing the work into lessons; the work should be tailored to your class.)

When you are ready to have a melody played on the bottles, you must not only have a player for each bottle but also a director. You may show the children how to direct the first few times. If a child is to be a director, he should practice ahead of time. The bottles to be used can be lined up on a table, spaced as if each was being held by a child. Place the table in front of the chalk board. The notes of the song should be written above the bottles on the board. The director should point to the bottles in the order of the notes of the song. For example, if the song chosen is "Hot Cross Buns," he would point to "mi," then "re" and "do; mi, re, do; do, do, do, do, re, re, re, re; mi, re, do." As soon as the child can do it in the proper rhythm and in the proper sequence, he may try it with the bottle blowers.

Ask the bottle blowers to line up behind the table in front of the chalk board. "Do" should be to the left. Always let the children figure out the order of the scale notes without help. The director faces the players and can see the song on the chalk board behind them. When he directs, he is actually "playing" on an "instrument" the way an orchestra conductor "plays" on his instrument, the orchestra. When the director points to a bottle player, that person blows on his bottle. He may use a ruler or a slender stick like a rhythm stick for a baton.

So that the children will know what they are supposed to do, the director might have the players play a scale up and down. Or he might improvise a short melody. Make it a rule that he always end his improvisation on high or low "do."

You will probably want to have every child participate. However, some of your young children will not have sufficient power to produce a tone on a bottle. Assure anyone who does not succeed that he will be able to do it either after more practice or after he has grown a little more. By the age of eight, a child usually can be expected to be able to blow a tone on a bottle. If there are more than eight good blowers, tune up another set of bottles. Otherwise, extra children can be singers, directors, players of rhythm band instruments or whatever is needed.

There are various ways to use bottles as instruments in the music lesson. If the song is "Hot Cross Buns," for instance, they could be used to play the song through as an introduction. Then everyone could sing it, and the bottles could be played again for an ending. Or, you could have the bottles play parts of tunes. For example, every time "E-I-E-I-O" is sung in the song, "Old Mac-Donald," the bottles could be played. Bottles could be used to play an ostinato for a song. (The section, *Harmonizing with an Ostinato*, starting on page 131 might give you song ideas.)

Review with the children what they have learned about sounds made by blowing and about pitch from these experiments.

When they were tuning the bottles, they should have learned to listen so as to match pitches. They will have found out how flute and piccolo players make sound on their instruments. If they were bottle players who helped make melody, they would have learned to follow a director. Those who had turns as director will have gained self assurance and learned how to lead others.

Experiments for Upper Grades. In the experiments for lower grades, bottles were tuned by displacing some of their air with water. However, when air is forced against a wall that consists partially of water, the resulting tone is impaired. Not only is the sound from an empty bottle superior; it is easier to produce.

With a lot of people helping it is possible to collect a set of bottles representing notes in a wide range of pitches. Small bottles that once contained flavoring extracts, Worcestershire sauce, soy sauce, etc. will make the highest sounds; quart juice bottles, large vinegar bottles, and the like will make the lowest.

You might begin by asking everyone in the class to bring in no more than a half dozen bottles, preferably unusual ones. Tell them that they must have small mouths. The owner or finder of each bottle should test it before he brings it in to make sure it has a good tone and is easy to play. Small identification labels will prevent mix-ups.

When you think there are enough bottles, bring them to the area of a piano. Have the children line them up by size. Do not discard any just because they look exactly like others. There is always a slight variation in pitch and in tone of bottles that appear to be the same.

Before starting to test bottles, tell the children that each one should play only on those that are his. Germs from colds and other infectious diseases can be spread if various people play the same bottle. If exchanges must be made, use some method of cleaning the rim of the mouth such as washing with soap and hot water, wiping with a rag soaked in mouthwash or medicinal alcohol, etc.

Instruct the children to make a tone on a bottle. The rim should be pressed against the chin under the lower lip and the upper lip should be thrust part way over the top, but not touching the rim. Air should be forced into the bottle to make sound. Because children may not be used to breathing out with force, they may feel lightheaded if they play for any length of time.

Have one child at the piano when the testing for notes begins. Start with the largest bottles. Have one of them played. The person at the piano should hunt among some of the lower-sounding notes until he finds one of the same pitch or close to it. The bottle should be given the letter name of the note.

If the children do not know the musical letter names of notes, give them the information they need. The white notes of the piano keyboard are named for the first seven letters of the alphabet. To know which note is which, we depend on the black notes. These are arranged in sets of two's and three's up and down the keyboard. A white note located just to the left of any two black notes is always one of the C's. This is an important note for all instrumentalists because the key of C is the least complicated to play. Playing with C's scale notes means for the pianist that he will probably not need to use any black notes.

Help the children find middle C. This is the C which is close to the middle of the keyboard. It is a note that can be sung quite easily by children's voices. Middle C is easily recognized in music writing. It is the note below the staff of the G clef with a line through it. Once the children know where C is on the piano, they will be able to name the other notes. The note to the right of C is D; the next note is E; then come F, G, A, B, and high C.

The black notes on the piano are the sharps and flats. The black note just to the right of a white note is the sharp (#) of that note. The black note to the left of a white note is its flat (b). Every black note can have two names. For example, the black note to the right of C is C#; it can also be D^b since it is just left of D.

As you and your children discover the pitch of each bottle by matching it to a note on the piano, you should label it in large letters one-and-a-half to two inches high. All bottles that sound like black notes will have two names: C#-D^b, D#-E^b, F#-G^b, G#-A^b, and A#-B^b. Tell the children that at the time a black note is being used, it will be called by only one, not both names. The name used will depend on the key in which the music is being sung or played.

In some cases it may be impossible to find a bottle in the exact pitch of a piano tone. In such cases choose a bottle which is just a shade lower than the pitch you want and add enough water to correct it. It is not necessary to have a set of bottles with all of the black notes. Try to find all of the white notes and F# and B^b. All notes that are below middle C should have a line under the letter (G̲, A̲, B̲, etc.). From middle C to the B above leave the letters plain. The notes high C and above should have a line over them (C̄, D̄, Ē, etc.)

When you assign children to play the various bottles, explain that many of them will not be playing a lot of the time because each song will have only a limited number of notes. Children assigned to the little-used notes—like C#, E♭, etc.—will be singing, directing, perhaps helping at the piano, or taking other roles. If you know who they are, have the best players on the most-used notes, like C, D, E, F, and G.

Choose a song from the Song Section, preferably a song everyone knows. Write the music on the chalk board at a place that will be above the children's heads. See which notes will be needed and choose a child who will not be playing a bottle to be the director. It is a good idea to give him time to practice before trying to direct the bottle players.

Place the bottles to be used for the song in order—the lowest always to the left—on a table in front of the chalk board. They should be under the music of the song with the letter names facing the room. The director should stand in front of them and practice by pointing to the appropriate bottles in turn.

When the director is ready, have the bottle players station themselves under the music on the board. Have the lowest note players stand behind those playing the notes in the normal voice range. If the notes to be used are C, D, E, G and A, those players will be in the front row. The players of C̲, D̲, E̲, G̲ and A̲ will stand directly behind them. All players must watch the director at all times and play when he points to them. They will be like members of an orchestra watching a conductor. Give other children turns at directing if they have practiced.

When having melody played on bottles, you could use the playing to introduce singing. The bottle players would play the melody through once, the singers would sing it, and perhaps the bottle players would play once more for a coda. Or, let the bottle players make a short introduction; then have them play while the singers sing. The kind of arrangement you will make will depend on the song.

Since you will probably have sets of bottles in two octaves, you could have the lower notes play harmony to the melody of the higher notes. See *Harmonizing with Vocal Chordings* which starts on page 147. The chordings can easily be done by bottle players. You would need two directors—one to direct the melody players, the other the harmony players. The harmony group and its director should stand to one side of the melody players. Melodies for all songs except "Silent Night" and the verse part of "Jingle Bells" are to be found in the Song Section of this chapter.

Bottle players can accompany other songs in the Song Section with chords. After a song has been chosen, find out how many different chords are needed for the accompaniment, and give each one a number. The note composition of each chord is given at the beginning of the section.

For example, "He's Got the Whole World in His Hands" has two chords—F and C_7. The F chord would be given the number 1; C_7 the number 2. You would find out that F, A and $\overline{C}$ are the notes of the F chord; C, E, G and B^b are the notes of the C_7 chord. You would have the players of bottles $\underline{F}$, $\underline{A}$ and C together and the players of $\underline{C}$, $\underline{E}$, $\underline{G}$ and $\underline{B}^b$ close by. If necessary, have the chord players practice by having the chord director point from one group to the other very slowly until everyone is accustomed to following the director's signals. The melody group would play the first three notes; then the harmony group would play with them.

Playing a Wind Instrument

School children are often given instruction in playing various inexpensive toy-like instruments, partly to give them musical enjoyment and partly to teach them to read music notes and help them appreciate all that is involved in playing a musical instrument. The tonette, song flute and flutophone have been among the more popular of the wind instruments studied.

The soprano recorder has also been taught in schools for the same reasons. It, too, is not expensive, though it may cost a little more than the others. It looks something like a small-sized clarinet, and it makes a tone like an orchestral instrument. It is superior to the other instruments because with it accurate intonation is possible. It can be played loud to soft, and its tone blends well with the human singing voice.

The recorder is an ancient instrument whose origins go back to the twelfth century. It was very popular in the time of Shakespeare, and Bach, Scarlatti and Handel are among the composers who wrote music for it. Since it is not a toy, the serious student can find music literature at an advanced level if he wishes to continue study. Not only is there recorder music from earlier centuries; much contemporary folk music sounds well on a recorder.

There are six sizes of recorder available, ranging from the large, low-toned great bass to the small piccolo-sized sopranino. Most popular are the soprano and the alto instruments, with tenor recorders next. Many towns and cities offer recorder instruction in adult education courses. It is not uncommon for families to own and play recorders in a variety of sizes as a pastime.

Could you learn to play a recorder and teach your children to play them? Yes. You run little risk of picking up bad habits that would prevent you from making good progress. To learn to play a piano or violin, for instance, most people need the guidance of a teacher. But only simple techniques are needed to play a recorder, techniques like using the proper amount of breath, tonguing to make tones clear, closing the holes completely with the fingers, listening for good tone, etc. For these reasons we recommend that you choose to teach your children the recorder.

The soprano recorder is a tube of wood or plastic twelve inches long and having a row of small holes. The mouthpiece is shaped to fit inside the player's mouth. Recorder study can be started any time from late second grade on; study can be continued at all grade levels, on into adulthood.

If the children in your school will eventually have the opportunity to learn to play band or orchestral instruments, the recorder can be used to awaken interest, to learn to read music, to learn ensemble playing, following directions, etc. By finding out that it is easy to produce a pleasant tone and play a melody, children should feel motivated to study more difficult instruments.

Ideally, every child in the classroom should have his own instrument. You could encourage anyone who was interested to purchase one and use school funds to outfit the others. If you had enough recorders on hand to loan one to every child, they could be sterilized at the end of the year for the next class. Each player should have his own study book. Find a way to label the player's name onto his instrument so that there are no mix-ups.

Plastic recorders are usually less expensive and require less care than do those made of wood. But the wooden instruments have superior tone. If the latter are used, give them special care. A wood recorder should be oiled with woodwind oil (available at a music instrument supply store) before its first use and then three or four times a year. The oil will dry in half a day. A wood recorder should be stored away from heat and dampness. It should never be kept in the sun, near hot radiators, etc. Since moisture from the player's mouth will inevitably accumulate in the core of the instrument during playing, each part should be swabbed with a wiper—a long-handled, soft-bristled brush, a clean rag, etc. Each instrument should be stored in a box, a canvas bag, or some kind of carrying case.

Start recorder lessons by helping children establish good habits. For the first lesson and each lesson thereafter, ask that everyone sit straight and give reminders from time to time during the lesson. If they are using wood recorders, the players should hold them in their hands for a few moments to warm them. Then the mouthpiece should be placed lightly between the lips, and the player should blow gently to get a tone. Next, have everyone take the instruments away from their mouths and, with lips slightly apart, whisper "tu." It will be a bit like lightly spitting. The mouthpiece should again be placed between the lips, and the players should try to tongue with "tu" and produce a tone. This can be practiced in spare time or at home, if you will allow instruments to be brought home. When the children think they can do it, have them do it individually for you. This is called tonguing.

Next, the players must practice covering the holes carefully. It is important to press the fingers in such a way that no air can pass. The children should know that the air will always go to the nearest opening. If no holes are covered, it will escape through the top hole. If all holes are covered, it will have to go the length of the instrument. Also, players should be warned not to rest fingers on holes that are not supposed to be covered.

The recorder method book which you will use will have instructions for introducing the notes and their fingerings one by one. You may find it useful to have cards showing the fingering of each note to which everyone can refer. You will need seventeen pieces of heavy paper like oak tag cut to about four by nine inches. Make a pattern of a picture of a recorder six inches long and an inch wide. Cut holes around which to trace. Center the pattern on each piece of oak tag, and make the tracings. As each new note is learned, fingerings can be blacked in. (Since the highest notes that can be played on a recorder are seldom used, you need not make cards for them unless the group is playing at an advanced level.)

If anyone is interested and if there is time to schedule it, have a recorder club which meets weekly to work on special music. Try a thirty-minute session with third and fourth graders, fifty minutes for fifth and sixth graders.

MAKING MELODY WITH PERCUSSION

Most percussion instruments produce tones of indefinite pitch. But the various kinds of bells, the bars of xylophones and marimbas, and the tuned timpani drums make tones of recognizable pitch. Some of these instruments can be modified sufficiently to make it easy for children to play simple melodies on them. If the instrument is the xylophone, for instance, the bars which will not be needed for a particular melody can be removed. Or, to simplify the task of playing a tune on resonator bells (tuned bell blocks), the player would be given only those bell blocks which are needed for the tune he is playing.

In recent years Carl Orff, the German composer, has done much to influence the direction of music education in the world. Because he believed that striking is a natural motion for children, he developed special percussion instruments of high quality on which they could play melody.

Orff was preceded by, and undoubtedly influenced by, an earlier European music educator, Jacques Dalcroze, who introduced rhythmic movement which he called eurythmics to music education. He felt it was essential that students move to a musical accompaniment.

A contemporary of Orff's, Zoltan Kodaly, was a Hungarian composer-educator who advocated that singing and movement be done simultaneously. Many of his ideas have been adopted by present-day music teachers. Orff and Kodaly undoubtedly influenced one another.

Kodaly had children learn to sing with so-fa syllables, and he had them learn a hand signal for each note. The notes were not to be introduced in scale order. Instead, he felt they should be learned in a sequence which children seem naturally to follow when they sing and chant while playing. "So mi" was to be learned first; then "la" was added. "Do" was next, followed by "re." "La so mi re do" are the notes of the pentatonic scale, about which we will learn later. "Fa" and "ti" were added last.

Like Kodaly, Orff wanted children to start by using only a few musical notes, those used with their calls, taunts and the chants of their playground games. During play, children in all parts of the world use the same few notes; these are the notes of the pentatonic scale. Most of the songs written by Orff use this five-toned scale; he encourages children to improvise with these notes.

Carl Orff's music education work has been mostly at the elementary level. He wanted children to move from spoken language to bodily movement to melody. Melody-making was to start at a small range and gradually become extended. Emphasis was on the rhythmic element of music over the melodic and harmonic.

Orff rhythms were to be intricate. He wanted children to use "body instruments"—hands for clapping or slapping thighs, feet for stamping, fingers for snapping—to express themselves rhythmically. And he wanted them to use rhythmic speech. He felt that music, movement and speech were inseparable for children. They were to be trained in singing, in playing an instrument, and in activities involving the whole body. Improvisation in dance was encouraged.

In the Orff system children are not only instructed in how to play on percussion instruments; they can also improvise on them. These instruments are of high quality, capable of producing superior tone. They are used both for melodies and accompaniments. One of the forms of accompaniment Orff liked is the ostinato, a form that was presented in Chapter 4.

About Orff Percussion Instruments

Since the early 1960's, American music educators have taken many of the teaching ideas of Orff and Kodaly and have adapted them to suit the American school child and American teaching philosophies. Those educators who have chosen to ignore them have objected to such things as the absence of the music of master composers, the use of a limited number of tones in improvisation that can result in boring music, the assumption that children are primarily interested in rhythm, sing-song singing, musical instruments that are played by striking, along with a lot of bodily movement, and the use of special musical instruments. Everyone would agree that these Orff instruments have excellent tone. Objections have arisen for other reasons.

First, catalogs show a bewildering variety of types and sizes of percussion instruments, many of which look and sound similar to others. There are several sizes of kettle drums, for instance. The timpani have cylindrical bodies, and all drums can be tuned to play any of five notes.

There are three kinds of "bar" instruments—glockenspiels, metallophones and xylophones. The first two types have metal bars; the xylophones have wooden bars. The metallophones and xylophones are made in several sizes, ranging from the largest (which play low tones) through medium-sized (called altos) to the smallest (called sopranos). Glockenspiels start at higher pitches and range from alto to high soprano.

Because they are expertly made, these instruments are very expensive. The smallest costs just under forty dollars; the largest over six hundred dollars. To support them, adjustable legs or tables of various heights can also be purchased. Or instruments can be placed on the floor, where players can sit and bend over them.

One of the great advantages of the Orff "bar" instruments is that every bar can be removed. This allows the teacher to leave only the few bars needed for a particular melody, and this removes the confusion of selecting the proper notes from a wide range of bars. It also makes improvisation on the instruments easy.

Because many school systems own one or more of the Orff percussion instruments, we will discuss ways to use them. However, it is not recommended that you purchase them. Instead, you could purchase a number of small, inexpensive xylophones with relatively good tone that can be used by a like number of children. To indicate which notes are not to be used, strips of heavy black paper can be used to blot out the bars not needed.

Another worthwhile purchase would be a set of resonator bells (also called tone educator bells, tuned bell blocks or tuned bells). These are tuned metal bars on blocks of wood. The bars are well supported for resonance, and the blocks are virtually indestructible. The tone of resonator bells is pleasant and blends well with singing voices.

Orff teaching methods can be used with these bells. With a single set of them it is possible to have a number of children taking part in an activity; a mallet is supplied for each bell block when a set is purchased. With Orff instruments only one person at a time can use an instrument. The resonator bells can be used by kindergarteners; they can be used and appreciated by children in every grade through high school.

Playing Percussion Instruments

Teach the children to play melody on percussion instruments by starting with something easy. The youngest children can play back and forth on two notes. Have the players look for the notes G and E. Tell them to be sure the longest bars are always to the left. They will be holding two mallets, one in the right hand, the other in the left.

Have the players practice playing G with the mallet in the right hand first. Tell them to hit the bar in such a way that the mallet bounces back. Wrists should be flexible. Next, have them play E with the mallet in the left hand. Have them go back and forth a few times on the two notes.

As soon as the players are well practiced, have everyone sing the following:

Everyone, including the players, should sing the song again; the players should sway to the right, then the left, keeping the rhythm of the notes. Next, everyone should sing and the players play the song. Finally, have the song played without any singing.

The song words can be changed and the song lengthened. Try: "Hey, there; I see you Tie-ing knots in Bob-by's shoe; What a fun-ny thing to do!"

As part of the Orff method the teacher and children embellish in imaginative ways whatever they are doing. For example, the song about rain could be played and sung with sound effects. There could be the swish of wind, the boom of thunder, the drip-drop of rain, the singing of the words, and the melody played on percussion instruments.

Have each part practiced first. Two or three maracas players would play in eighth-note rhythm to imitate the wind. Someone could play a low-pitched drum, making a single boom once every four beats. A half-dozen pairs of rhythm sticks could make a light-sounding tick, tick, tick, tick to imitate dripping rain. Small xylophones, resonator blocks or Orff instruments would play the tune through as introduction, as accompaniment to the singing, and as a coda after the singing.

When everyone is ready, position players so that they can watch you for signals. Have the maracas players start with the faint hiss of wind for about two measures. Point to the drum player for a clap of thunder. Let the maracas play again, this time a little louder. While they keep going, rhythm sticks lightly tick to imitate the beginning of the rain. They play louder as the rain increases. The melody instruments are added; they play the song through. Everyone continues and the singers sing the song. (Since it is short, they could sing it twice.) The melody players play one more time and stop. The rhythm sticks stop. Maracas stop. The music ends with one more clap of thunder.

Older children can have similar experiences. Choose a song from the Song Section that has few notes. Be sure everyone knows how to sing it. Teach the melody players to play the notes. Then make some kind of an arrangement combining singers and players.

Suppose, for example, the song chosen is "Scotland's Burning." The music for this is in Chapter 3, and the children may already have learned to sing it as a round. Have the song reviewed. Then assign children to play small xylophones, resonator bells, or Orff instruments. The notes needed will be D G A B and $\overline{\text{D}}$. Those with instruments with removable bars should take off the bars that will not be needed. With both hands holding onto each bar, they can be instructed to remove C, E, F, $\overline{\text{C}}$, etc. Those instruments with permanently fixed bars should have the same bars covered with heavy black paper. Each player of resonator bells should be given the five bells needed and should line them up with the longest bar to the left.

Teach the instrument players to play the song phrase by phrase. They should listen while everyone sings the first phrase—D, D, G, G, D, D, G, G. Ask them to play it. (They should hear without being told that the two notes needed will be the lowest note which is farthest to the left and the next one over to the right.) Have the second phrase sung—A, B, A, B. This should be played. The third phrase is sung—$\overline{\text{D}}$, $\overline{\text{D}}$, $\overline{\text{D}}$, $\overline{\text{D}}$—and played. When the fourth phrase is sung, ask the children to tell you the other phrase exactly like it. (The first phrase has the same notes.) Have the instrument players play the song the whole way through.

Think of an imaginative way to present the song. A gong could represent the gong of a fire engine, and triangles could chime to add to the excitement. Scrapers and shakers, jingle sticks, cymbals, etc. can be used effectively. Ask the children to help think of ways to play such instruments during the singing of the song and playing of the melody instruments.

Start the presentation quietly, as if the fire is just starting. A few crackles might be heard first. Have the scrapers play a few times, perhaps a quarter-note-and-rest pattern. Add the shakers in the same pattern to gradually increase the volume. The jingle sticks could be shaken in eighth-note rhythm, and a pair of cymbals could crash ominously. Melody players play the tune on their instruments, and on "Fire, fire, fire, fire," the gong and triangles join them. Everyone should repeat the melody with singers singing once or twice. They should stop, and melody players play again (with gong and triangles chiming in). The music should quiet down with jingle sticks stopping first and then the shakers and finally the scrapers stopping. Let different children direct the players and singers, each in a different way until you find an arrangement that pleases everyone.

You will find many children's poems that can be chanted on the sing-song "so, mi" or "so, mi, la, so, mi." The latter tune is the one children use to tease each other: "Frannie has a boy friend!" or "I've got Albert's notebook—And I'm going to read it!" Find short, rhythmical poems about such subjects as cowboys whose horses are galloping, about children who are skipping, etc., and have them sung, then played on melody instruments.

When you have a number of melody percussion instruments, some can play melody while others accompany it. You can give specific instructions for the accompaniments, perhaps a short pattern of notes played in one rhythm, a second instrument being played with the two mallets striking two notes simultaneously, and a third having the two mallets play back and forth on two notes. You can have an instrument played every time a particular word or phrase is sung. With Orff methods you can lead children to improvise accompaniments on their percussion melody instruments.

Improvisation: Using the Pentatonic Scale

The pentatonic (five-toned) scale dates back four thousand years. It was also used in medieval times and has been used by such diverse cultures as the American Indian, the Chinese and some Africans. American spirituals like "Swing Low, Sweet Chariot" and "Nobody Knows the Trouble I've Seen" and American folk songs like "Old MacDonald," "Cindy" and "Barnyard Song" ("I Bought Me a Cat") use the notes of the pentatonic. Both Orff and Kodaly have revived use of this scale in their work with school children.

Most of the music of the western world with which we are most familiar is composed with the notes of the diatonic major or minor scale. These scales have seven different notes ranging over the span of an octave. The seven notes must be placed closer together than the five notes of the pentatonic (from the Greek "pente tonos," meaning "five tones"). To hear what a pentatonic scale sounds like, play a set of five black notes on the piano. Play successively a group of three and, moving right, play the next group of two. Add the first note of the next group of three to complete the octave.

Because the pentatonic scale notes are spaced farther apart than the diatonic, they sound harmonious when sounded together in any combination. This makes it possible to have percussion instruments that can be reduced to these five tones—by removal of bars, by blotting out bars, by not including bell blocks—improvise an accompaniment to a melody which is also in the pentatonic.

There is more than one way of having children play songs using the five notes of the pentatonic scale. One is to have them use the black notes of the piano or the same notes on xylophones, Orff instruments, or resonator bells. (These are the notes C#, D#, F#, G#, A# or, as known by their other names, D^b, E^b, G^b, A^b, B^b.)

Suppose the song chosen is "Old MacDonald Had a Farm." Tell instrument players which notes to cover or which to use or not use. (It is easy to see the black notes on a piano and almost equally as easy to locate the groups of two's and three's on bar instruments with chromatic notes. Resonator bell blocks are labeled.)

Melody players should start on F# (G^b) and find the notes by ear. (Children may attempt this in their free time to prepare for the music lesson.) If the piano is used, a second child may make up a two- or three-note pattern using black notes below where the melody player is playing; a third child may create an accompaniment on the higher black notes of the piano.

The same combination of melody player with two- or three-note patterns of accompaniment can be tried with the other instruments.

Another way to have children use the pentatonic scale is to give more definite directions. Try "Old MacDonald Had a Farm" this way. Have the players prepare the instruments. They should remove middle C, F and $\overline{C}$. (Higher and lower instruments remove all F's and all C's.) The players of resonator bells should be given D, E, G, A and B. Small xylophone players should cover the C and F bars.

Melody players will learn to play the song by ear, starting on G. Assign someone to play the ostinato pattern suggested on page 133 of this book. (He should play the first measure once and the second measure three times.) Tell him to use the mallet in the right hand every time he plays G and E; the mallet in the left hand will always be used to play D. Instruct him to play G three times. Next, play D E E D. Repeat E E D twice. Ask him to tell you which part of the song sounds like the first part of what he is playing. He should tell you that it sounds like the first line of the song.

Ask a second player to play G with the mallet in his right hand and $\underline{B}$ with the mallet in his left hand. He should sound both notes together and repeat them slowly, once every two beats. A third player can be instructed to play the notes for the words "E-I-E-I-O" every time they are sung. This player would start on B and play B B A A with the mallet in the right hand, G with the mallet in the left.

A fourth player could play a high-pitched eighth-note pattern. Tell him to play $\overline{D}$ $\overline{E}$ back and forth lightly, using the two mallets. A fifth player can play low tones slowly. He could make two combinations: $\underline{G}$ and D, followed by $\underline{G}$ and E repeated throughout the song.

A good way to practice with the various players is to have each one start to play in turn and on signal from you. After all parts are playing correctly, bring in the singers, the melody player(s), and the "E-I-E-I-O" player. If this procedure is too complicated for younger students, have each part practice alone with the singers before putting it all together.

Have you ever watched an orchestra conductor and wished secretly that you were he, with your thin stick magically commanding a large assembly of people to play music on their instruments? Perhaps you were not jealous of his power; maybe you were impressed with the beauty of sound that resulted from the concerted effort of all participants. Whatever the motivation, it is now within the realm of possibility that you will be able to lead the members of your class in improvisations that will resemble the kind of playing done by an orchestra.

Improvisation in music was popular until the nineteenth century. Carl Orff and other contemporaries are largely responsible for the current interest in musical improvisation. To do it successfully the leader must feel free to try almost anything. No two improvisations will ever be the same; this is a little frightening to some people, but challenging to others. If instrumental players all use the notes of the pentatonic scale, they can play anything, and it will sound harmonious. They can be led by a complete novice who improvises in what he asks of the players. Most grownups and many children, especially those with an inclination to dramatize, make good conductors.

Improvisations should be done for fun, but you can make a few plans and decisions before starting one. For instance, you should place children where you can see them and they can see you. Line up those who will play certain rhythm instruments, those who will play the various melody instruments and singers. Also, have melody players prepare their instruments to play only the notes of the pentatonic scale. Tell everyone to watch you. You will signal them to start, indicate how fast they should go, how soft or loud to play, when to stop, when to start again, etc. Players on the melody instruments may play any notes, as long as they are following your directions.

Decide on one of the songs from the Song Section that is in the pentatonic scale and that everyone knows, and tell singers to be ready.

Here is one way you might do an improvisation without rehearsal beforehand. Start by pointing to the player of one of the stronger rhythm instruments, like drum, gong or cymbal. Indicate that he should play one loud sound, as if to announce that something is about to happen and everyone should pay attention. Wait and signal the player once again.

Next, turn to the players of some of the lighter rhythm instruments, like maracas or rhythm sticks. Move your hand in a steady rhythm to indicate that you want them to play a steady beat. When this is well established, move your hand up and down only slightly to indicate that they should continue playing softly; put the forefinger of your other hand to your lips as if to say: "Shh!" Point to one of the melody instruments and let him play an improvisation strongly. Then indicate that he should stop. Have a second melody instrument play a solo and stop. Have a few brief solos by the various melody instruments. Then have all the playing stopped and ask the singers to sing the song.

When the song has ended, let the rhythm players start again. Bring in the first melody player. Indicate that he should keep playing while the second player joins him. Continue to have the melody percussion players join in until everyone is playing. Then drop your hands suddenly to "cut" the playing altogether. Wait a moment and let everyone start again on signal. Again, "cut" the playing, and again have it started up.

Next, working backward, have each instrument stop playing in the reverse order in which it started, ending with the rhythm makers. Then have the strong instrument (drum, gong or cymbal) play a resounding tone. Wait. Have it played one more time softly, as if to say "The End."

SONG SECTION

The songs for this section have been selected for the beginner who wants to play melodies on a musical instrument. Most of the songs chosen are familiar and well-liked by people of all ages. To insure that the player succeed from the start, he should try music with a minimum of different notes. If possible, the notes should make a systematic pattern which is easy to figure out. For example, they might "step" up or down in a scalewise pattern; if there are "skips," the pattern of those that are the same distance will be easiest to figure out; a pattern of repeated notes is also easy to see. Encourage children to learn slowly, to speed up later.

You will notice that the letter and syllable names of notes are given only the first time a note appears in the music. For instance, if the sequence is "C C G G A A G" or, in syllables, "do do so so la la so," only the first C (do), the first G (so), and the first A (la) will be written. The children should figure out the repeated notes.

If you and your children built a monochord or if you have a one-stringed instrument, you will use letter names for the notes. The bottle players in the upper grades will have matched the pitches of bottles to notes on the piano, and they will need letter names. If your students are learning the recorder or other small wind instrument, they will have study books; they will be able to play the songs in this section, also. To play percussion instruments—xylophones, resonator bells, Orff instruments, etc.—letter names will be needed.

Children in lower grades will be tuning bottles to the scale they have learned to sing with so-fa syllables, and they should call the notes by those names.

If upper-grade children collected bottles which sound the pitches of sharps and flats, you can give them opportunities to play these bottles by choosing songs which contain them. Percussion players will have bars representing the sharps and flats.

All songs using the notes of the pentatonic scale can be played using the same notes as sharped (or flatted) notes. Here is how to do it. Find a song written with the pentatonic notes that is in the key of F and change all notes to sharps; F will be F#, G will become G#, etc. If the song in the pentatonic is in the key of G, change all notes to flats. G will be G^b, A will be A^b, and so forth.

The letters that appear above the notes of some songs are the chords for accompaniment. In this chapter it has been suggested that a set of tuned bottles in a lower octave could be used to play chords while bottles pitched at singing range play melody. The note composition of chords needed for these songs is given below.

Chord Composition

Chord name:	$C_{(7)}$	D_7	F	$G_{(7)}$	$\underline{B}^b$
Chord notes:	(B^b)	C		$(\bar{F})$	
	G	A	$\bar{C}$	$\bar{D}$	F
	E	F#	A	B	D
	C	D	F	G	$\underline{B}^{b'}$

Songs Using Three Notes

HOT CROSS BUNS

Tra litional

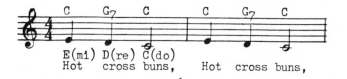

One a pen-ny, two a pen-ny, Hot cross buns.

MAKE MONDAY FUN DAY

J.L. Reynolds

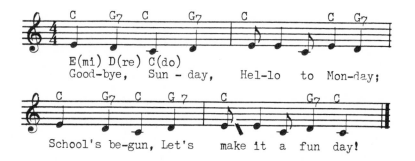

E(mi) D(re) C(do)
Good-bye, Sun - day, Hel-lo to Mon-day;

School's be-gun, Let's make it a fun day!

JUST MY LUCK

J.L. Reynolds

C(do) E(mi) D(re)
1. Just my luck! Walk-ing down the street,

Felt a cat, black and fat, Run a-cross my feet.

2. Just my luck! Fishing that same day;
   Pulled a trout—almost out, But he got away.

3. Just my luck! Friend said, "Don't despair;
   With a grin—you can win; Luck is ev'rywhere."

Songs Using Four Notes

MERRILY WE ROLL ALONG
(Tune: MARY HAD A LITTLE LAMB)

Traditional

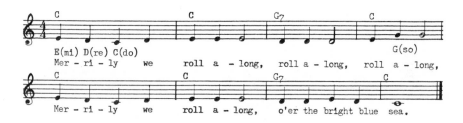

E(mi) D(re) C(do)
Mer – ri – ly   we   roll a – long, roll a – long, roll a – long,

G(so)

Mer – ri – ly   we   roll a – long,   o'er the bright blue   sea.

CHIMES OF BIG BEN
(For percussion instruments)

A   F   G   C

Other Songs Using Four Notes:

I LOVE COFFEE–Words, page 126. Key of G. *First note:* D (so). *Notes needed:* D E F# G (so la ti do)

RING AROUND A ROSY–Key of C. *First note:* G (so). *Notes needed:* E G A C̄ (mi so la d̄o)

TAPS–Key of G. *First note:* D (so). *Notes needed:* D G B D̄ (so do mi s̄o)

TICK TOCK–Words and music, page 101. Key of C. *First note:* C (do). *Notes needed:* C E G C̄ (do mi so d̄o)

Songs Using Five Notes

WHEN THE SAINTS GO MARCHING IN

Louisiana Marching Song

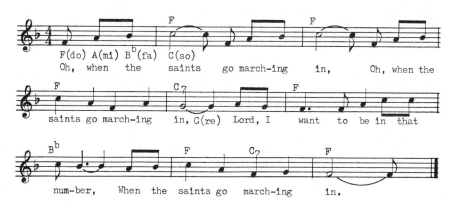

PETER, PETER, PUMPKIN EATER

Pentatonic Song   Old Tune

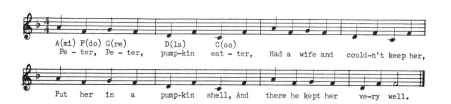

OLD MACDONALD HAD A FARM

Pentatonic Song   Traditional

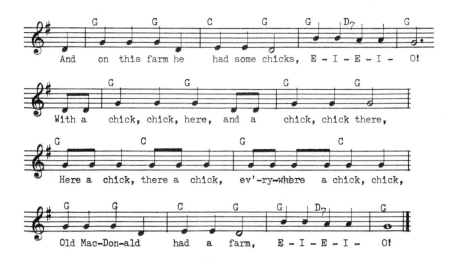

2. .....some ducks.....(quack, quack)

3. .....some turkeys.....(gobble, gobble)

4. .....some pigs.....(oink, oink)

5. .....a truck.....(rattle, rattle)

Other Songs Using Five Notes:

GET ON BOARD–*Pentatonic Song.* Key of F (or F#*). First note:* A (A#) (mi).
   Notes needed: C D F G A (C# D# F# G# A#) (so la do re mi)

GO TELL AUNT RHODIE–Words, page 125. Key of F. *First note:* A (mi).
   Notes needed: F G A B♭ C̄ (do re mi fa s̄o)

JINGLE BELLS (Chorus only)–Words, page 152. Key of G. *First note:* B (mi).
   Notes needed: G A B C̄ D̄ (do re mi f̄a s̄o)

LIGHTLY ROW–Key of C. *First note:* G (so). *Notes needed:* C D E F G (do re
   mi fa so)

LITTLE TOM TINKER–Words and music, page 101. Key of C. *First note:* C
   (do). *Notes needed:* C D E G C̄ (do re mi so d̄o)

THE LONE STAR TRAIL–Words, page 128. Key of F. *First note:* C (so). *Notes
   needed:* C F G A C̄ (so do re mi s̄o)

OATS AND BEANS AND BARLEY GROW–Key of G. *First note:* B (mi).
   Notes needed: G A B C̄ D̄ (do re mi f̄a s̄o)

OLD DAN TUCKER—*Pentatonic Song.* Key of F (or F#). *First note:* F (F#) (do). *Notes needed:* C D F G A (C# D# F# G# A#) (so la do re mi)

THE OLD GRAY MARE (First four phrases)—Words, page 131. Key of F. *First note:* C (so). *Notes needed:* C E F G A (so ti do re mi)

SCOTLAND'S BURNING—Words and music, page 106. Key of G. *First note:* D (so). *Notes needed:* D G A B D̄ (so do re mi sō)

Songs Using Six Notes

GOOD-BYE, OLD PAINT

Pentatonic Song   Cowboy Song

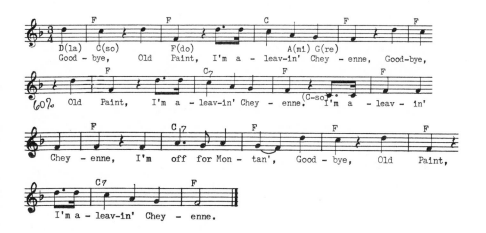

TWINKLE, TWINKLE, LITTLE STAR
(BAA, BAA, BLACK SHEEP)

Traditional

LONG, LONG AGO

T.H. Bayly

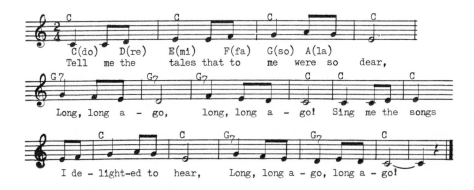

Other Songs Using Six Notes

ANGEL BAND–*Pentatonic Song.* Key of F (or F#). *First note:* C (C#) (so). *Notes needed:* C D F G A $\overline{\text{C}}$ (C# D# F# G# A# $\overline{\text{C}}$#) (so la do re mi $\overline{\text{so}}$)

AU CLAIRE DE LA LUNE–Key of G. *First note:* G (do). *Notes needed:* D E F# G A B (so la ti do re mi)

BARNYARD SONG (I BOUGHT ME A CAT)–*Pentatonic Song.* Key of C. *First note:* G (so). *Notes needed:* C D E G A $\overline{\text{C}}$ (do re mi so la $\overline{\text{do}}$)

FARMER IN THE DELL–*Pentatonic Song.* Key of F (or F#). *First note:* C (C#) (so). *Notes needed:* C F G A $\overline{\text{C}}$ $\overline{\text{D}}$ (C# F# G# A# $\overline{\text{C}}$# $\overline{\text{D}}$#) (so do re mi $\overline{\text{so}}$ $\overline{\text{la}}$)

FOR HE'S A JOLLY GOOD FELLOW–Words, page 150. Key of F. *First note:* F (do). *Notes needed:* F G A B$^\flat$ $\overline{\text{C}}$ $\overline{\text{D}}$ (do re mi fa $\overline{\text{so}}$ $\overline{\text{la}}$)

KUM BA YAH–Words, page 151. Key of D. *First note:* D (do). *Notes needed:* D E F# G A B (do re mi fa so la)

LI'L 'LIZA JANE—*Pentatonic Song.* Key of C. *First note:* E (mi) *Notes needed:* C D E G A C̄ (do re mi so la dō)

LONDON BRIDGE—Words, page 125. Key of F. *First note:* C̄ (sō). *Notes needed:* F G A B♭ C̄ D̄ (do re mi fa sō̄ lā)

LOVELY EVENING—Words and music, page 111. Key of F. *First note:* F (do). *Notes needed:* F G A B♭ C̄ D̄ (do re mi fa sō̄ lā)

MARY WORE A RED DRESS—*Pentatonic Song.* Key of F (or F#). *First note:* C (C#) (so). *Notes needed:* C D F G A C̄ (C# D# F# G# A# C̄#) (so la do re mi sō̄)

OH, SUSANNA—Words, page 137. Key of F. *First note:* F (do). *Notes needed:* F G A B♭ C̄ D̄ (do re mi fa sō̄ lā)

ROW, ROW, ROW YOUR BOAT—Words and music, page 106. Key of C. *First note:* C (do). *Notes needed:* C D E F G C̄ (do re mi fa so dō)

SKIP TO MY LOU—Words, page 125. Key of F. *First note:* A (mi). *Notes needed:* E F G A B♭ C̄(ti do re mi fa sō̄)

THIS OLD MAN Key of F. *First note:* C̄ (sō). *Notes needed:* F G A B♭ C̄ D̄ (do re mi fa sō̄ lā)

TOODALA—*Pentatonic Song.* Key of F (or F#). *First note:* C (C#) (so). *Notes needed:* C D F G A C̄ (C# D# F# G# A# C̄#) (so la do re mi sō̄)

Songs Using Seven Notes

AULD LANG SYNE

Pentatonic Song   Scotch Tune

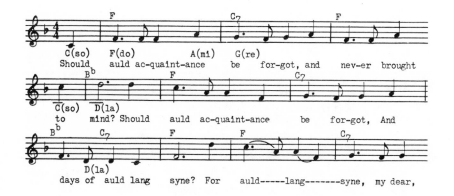

For   auld-----lang--------syne,   We'll   take   a   cup   o'   kind-ness yet,

For   auld-----lang-------   syne.

AMERICA

Henry Carey

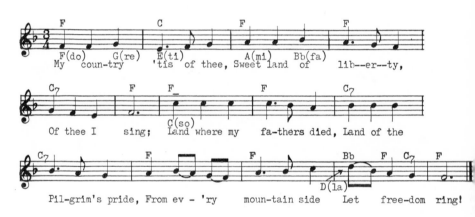

My   coun-try   'tis   of thee, Sweet land of   lib--er--ty,

Of thee I   sing;   Land where my   fa-thers died, Land of the

Pil-grim's pride, From ev - 'ry   moun-tain side   Let   free-dom   ring!

THE MORE WE GET TOGETHER

German Folk Song

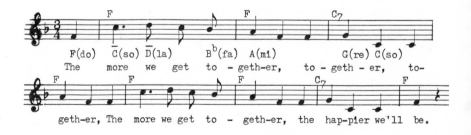

The   more   we   get   to - geth-er,   to - geth - er,   to-

geth-er, The   more   we get   to - geth-er,   the   hap-pier we'll   be.

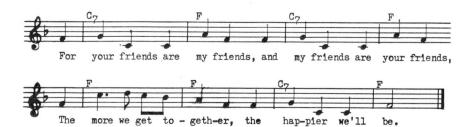

For your friends are my friends, and my friends are your friends,

The more we get to - geth-er, the hap-pier we'll be.

Other Songs Using Seven Notes:

ARE YOU SLEEPING?—Words and Music, page 104. Key of E^b. *First note:* E^b (do). *Notes needed:* $\underline{B}^b$ E^b F G A^b B^b $\overline{C}$ (so do re mi fa so $\overline{la}$)

DOWN IN THE VALLEY—Words, page 141. Key of G. *First note:* D (so). *Notes needed:* D F# G A B $\overline{C}$ $\overline{D}$ (so ti do re mi fa so)

FOR HEALTH AND STRENGTH—Words and music, page 108. Key of F. *First note:* C(so). *Notes needed:* C E F G A B^b $\overline{C}$ (so ti do re mi fa so)

LEAVIN' OLD TEXAS—Words and music, page 113. *Pentatonic song.* Key of F (or F#). *First note:* C (C#) (so). *Notes needed:* C D F G A $\overline{C}$ $\overline{D}$ (C# D# F# G# A# $\overline{C}$# $\overline{D}$#) (so la do re mi so la)

HE'S GOT THE WHOLE WORLD IN HIS HANDS—Words, page 128. Key of F. *First note:* $\overline{C}$ (so). *Notes needed:* E F G A B^b $\overline{C}$ $\overline{D}$ (ti do re mi fa so la)

SHOO, FLY—Words, page 127. Key of G. *First note:* B (mi). *Notes needed:* D F# G A B $\overline{C}$ $\overline{D}$ (so ti do re mi fa so)

SWING LOW, SWEET CHARIOT—*Pentatonic song.* Key of F (or F#). *First note:* A (A#) (mi). *Notes needed:* C D F G A $\overline{C}$ $\overline{D}$ (C# D# F# G# A# $\overline{C}$# $\overline{D}$#) (so la do re mi so la)

THREE BLIND MICE—Words and music, page 105. Key of E^b. *First note:* G(mi). *Notes needed:* E^b F G A^b B^b $\overline{D}$ $\overline{E}^b$ (do re mi fa so ti do)

TRAIN IS A-COMING—Words, page 133. *Pentatonic Song.* Key of D. *First note:* D (do). *Notes needed:* $\underline{B}$ D E F# A B $\overline{D}$ (la do re mi so la do)

TURN THE GLASSES OVER—*Pentatonic song.* Key of F (or F#). *First note:* F (F#) (do). *Notes needed:* C D F G A $\overline{C}$ $\overline{D}$ (C# D# F# G# A# $\overline{C}$# $\overline{D}$#) (so la do re mi so la)

Songs Using Eight Notes

CINDY

Pentatonic Song   Southern Tune

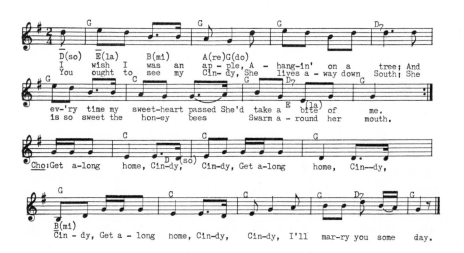

FESTIVAL DAY CHIMES
(For percussion instruments)

Other Songs Using Eight Notes

HOME ON THE RANGE—Words, page 141. Key of F. *First note:* C (so). *Notes needed:* C D E F G A B^b $\overline{C}$ (so la ti do re mi fa $\overline{so}$)

JOY TO THE WORLD–Key of C. *First note:* $\overline{C}$ ($\overline{do}$). *Notes needed:* C D E F G A B $\overline{C}$ (do re mi fa so la ti $\overline{do}$)

LITTLE DAVID–Words, page 128. *Pentatonic song.* Key of F. (or F#). *First note:* A (A# (mi). *Notes needed:* C D F G A $\overline{C}$ $\overline{D}$ $\overline{F}$ (C# D# F# G# A# $\overline{C}$# $\overline{D}$# $\overline{F}$# (so la do re mi $\overline{so}$ $\overline{la}$ $\overline{do}$)

O COME, ALL YE FAITHFUL–Key of F. *First note:* F (do). *Notes needed:* C D E F G A B^b $\overline{C}$ (so la ti do re mi fa $\overline{so}$)

SOURCE MATERIALS FOR MUSIC LESSONS

Following are names and addresses of companies which can supply materials for music lessons:

BASIC ELEMENTARY MUSIC TEXTS

Birchard Music Series, 1958-1962
  Summy-Birchard Company
  1834 Ridge Avenue
  Evanston, Illinois 60304

Discovering Music Together, 1966
  Follett Publishing Company
  1010 West Washington Boulevard
  Chicago, Illinois 60607

Exploring Music, 1966
  Holt, Rinehart and Winston, Inc.
  383 Madison Avenue
  New York, N.Y. 10017

Growing with Music, 2nd Edition, 1966
  Prentice-Hall, Inc.
  Englewood Cliffs, New Jersey 07632

The Magic of Music, 1965-1968
  Ginn and Company
  191 Spring Street
  Lexington, Massachusetts 02173

Music for Young Americans, 2nd Edition, 1966
  American Book Company
  300 Pike Street
  Cincinnati, Ohio 45202

Silver Burdett Music, 1974
  Silver Burdett Division
  General Learning Corporation
  Morristown, New Jersey 07960

The Spectrum of Music, 1974
  MacMillan Publishing Co., Inc.
  200 F Brown Street
  Riverside, New Jersey 08075

This Is Music, 2nd Edition, 1967-1968
  Allyn and Bacon, Inc.
  470 Atlantic Avenue
  Boston, Massachusetts 02210

CATALOG SOURCES FOR BELLS, SMALL XYLOPHONES, AND OTHER MELODY PERCUSSION INSTRUMENTS

1. Basic Distributors
   1137 Seventh Avenue
   San Diego, California 92011

2. Harmolin
   P.O. Box 244
   La Jolla, California 92037

3. Kitching Educational
   Division of Ludwig Industries
   1728 N. Damen Ave.
   Chicago, Illinois 60647

4. Peripole Products, Inc.
   51-17 Rockaway Beach Boulevard
   Far Rockaway, N.Y. 11691

5. Rhythm Band, Inc.
   P.O. Box 126
   Fort Worth, Texas 76101

6. Scientific Music Industries, Inc.
   1055 South Wabash Avenue
   Chicago, Illinois 60805

7. Targ & Dinner, Inc.
   2451 N. Sacramento Ave.
   Chicago, Illinois 60647

8. Walberg and Ange
   86 Mechanic Street
   Worcester, Massachusetts 01608

9. David Wexler & Company
   823 South Wabash Avenue
   Chicago, Illinois 60605

CATALOG SOURCES FOR RECORDS

"Dance-a-Story" records available from:
   Ginn and Company
   191 Spring Street
   Lexington, Massachusetts 02173

RCA Victor
   "Rhythm Bands" album available from:
   RCA Victor Educational Sales
   155 East 24th Street
   New York, N.Y. 10010

CATALOG SOURCES FOR RECORDERS

1. Hargail Music, Inc.
   28 West 38th Street
   New York, N.Y. 10018

2. Jensen Manufacturing Division
   The Muter Company
   6601 South Laramie Avenue
   Chicago, Illinois 60638

3. Kitching Educational
   Division of Ludwig Industries
   1728 N. Damen Avenue
   Chicago, Illinois 60647

4. Trophy Music Company
   1278 West 9th Street
   Cleveland, Ohio 44113

CATALOG SOURCES FOR RHYTHM INSTRUMENTS

1. C. Bruno & Son, Inc.
   55 Marcus Drive
   Melville, New York 11746

2. Lyons, Inc.
   223 West Lake Street
   Chicago, Illinois 60606

3. Magnamusic-Baton, Inc.
   6390 Delmar Boulevard
   St. Louis, Missouri 63130

4. Peripole Products, Inc.
   51-17 Rockaway Beach Boulevard
   Far Rockaway, N.Y. 11691

5. Rhythm Band, Inc.
   P.O. Box 126
   Fort Worth, Texas 76101

BIBLIOGRAPHY

d'Auberge, Alfred and Manus, Morton: *It's Recorder Time.* New York, N.Y.: Alfred Music Company, Inc., 1968.

Burakoff, Gerald and Sonya: *The Classroom Recorder.* Hicksville, N.Y.: Consort Music, Inc., 1970.

McLaughlin and Dawley: *Make Music with the Bells.* (Carl Van Roy Company) Distributed by Peripole Products, Inc., Far Rockaway, New York.

Olenick, Elmer: *Lessons for the Soprano Recorder,* Book I, Book II and Teacher's Guides. Available from Jensen Manufacturing Division of The Muter Company, Chicago, Illinois.

Trapp Family: *Enjoy Your Recorder.* Sharon, Connecticut: Magnamusic Distributors, Inc., 1954.

Wheeler, Lawrence and Elizabeth: *An Elementary Guide for Learning the Recorder, Singing and Playing with Orff Instrumentation.* Melville, N.Y.: Belwin Mills Publishing Corporation, 1972.

White, Florence and Bergmani, Anni: *Playing the Recorder.* New York, N.Y.: Edward B. Marks Corporation, 1955.

INDEX